THE SONG CELESTIAL

THE SONG CELESTIAL

OR

BHAGAVAD-GITA
(FROM THE MAHABHARATA)

*Being a Discourse Between Arjuna,
Prince of India, and the Supreme Being
Under the Form of Krishna*

TRANSLATED FROM THE SANSKRIT TEXT
BY

SIR EDWIN ARNOLD
M.A., K.C.I.E., C.S.I.

Self-Realization Fellowship
Los Angeles, California
1977

ISBN 0-87612-210-1

Printed in the United States of America

2079-377-8M

DEDICATION

To India

इत्यहं वासुदेवस्य पार्थस्य च महात्मनः ।
संवादमिममश्रौषमद्भुतं रोमहर्षणं ॥
इति इह ज्ञानमाख्यातं गुह्याद्गुह्यतरं मया ।
तेभ्यस् न मे सिन्धो त्वदन्यः प्रियतरो भुवि ॥

So have I read this wonderful and spirit-
* thrilling speech,*
By Krishna and Prince Arjun held, discours-
* ing each with each;*
So have I writ its wisdom here, its hidden
* mystery,*
For England; O our India! as dear to me as
* She!*

EDWIN ARNOLD

PREFACE

This famous and marvelous Sanskrit poem occurs as an episode of the *Mahabharata*, in the sixth—or *"Bishma"*—Parva of the great Hindu epic. It enjoys immense popularity and authority in India, where it is reckoned as one of the "Five Jewels"—*pancharatnani*—of Devanagari literature. In plain but noble language it unfolds a philosophical system which remains to this day the prevailing Brahmanic belief, blending as it does with the doctrines of Kapila, Patanjali, and the Vedas. So lofty are many of its declarations, so sublime its aspirations, so pure and tender its piety, that Schlegel, after his study of the poem, breaks forth into this outburst of delight and praise towards its unknown author: *"Magistorum reverentia a Brachmanis inter sanctissima pietatis officia refertur. Ergo te primum, Vates sanctissime, Numinisque hypopheta! quisquis tandem inter mortales dictus tu fueris, carminis jujus auctor, cujus oraculis mens ad excelsa quaeque aeterna atque divina, cum inenarrabili quadam delectatione rapitur—te primum, inquam, salvere jubeo, et vestigia tua semper adoro."* Lassen re-echoes this splendid tribute; and indeed, so striking are some of the moralities here inculcated, and so close the parallelism—ofttimes actually verbal—between its teachings and those of the New Testament, that a controversy has arisen between Pandits and Missionaries on the point whether the author borrowed from Christian sources, or the Evangelists and Apostles from him.

This raises the question of its date, which cannot be positively settled. It must have been inlaid into the ancient epic at a period other than that of the original *Mahabharata*, but Mr. Kasinath Telang has offered

---

*"Among the holiest observances of piety noted down by the Brahmins is reverence toward the masters. I wish, therefore, to salute thee first, most holy prophet and interpreter of the Divinity, whosoever thou hast been said to be among mortals, author of that poem the prophetic sayings of which carry the mind with certain unerring delight to all that is lofty, eternal, and divine—and I worship forever thy footsteps." (Publisher's Note)

some fair argument to prove it anterior to the Christian era. The weight of evidence, however, tends to place its composition at about the third century after Christ; and perhaps there are really echoes in this Brahmanic poem of the lesson of Galilee, and of the Syrian incarnation.*

Its scene is the level country between the Jumna and the Sarsooti rivers—now Kurnal and Jheend. Its simple plot consists of a dialogue held by Prince Arjuna, the brother of King Yudhisthira, with Krishna, the Supreme Deity, wearing the disguise of a charioteer. A great battle is impending between the armies of the Kauravas and Pandavas, and this conversation is maintained in a war chariot drawn up between the opposing hosts.

The poem has been turned into French by Burnouf, into Latin by Lassen, into Italian by Stanislav Gatti, into Greek by Galanos, and into English by Mr. Thomson and

*Although this was the belief of scholars in the late nineteenth century, scholars nowadays generally agree that its origin precedes by several centuries the Christian era. (Publisher's Note)

Mr. Davies, the prose transcript of the last-named being truly beyond praise for its fidelity and clearness. Mr. Telang has also published at Bombay a version in colloquial rhythm, eminently learned and intelligent, but not conveying the dignity or grace of the original. If I venture to offer a translation of the wonderful poem after so many superior scholars, it is in grateful recognition of the help derived from their labors and because English literature would certainly be incomplete without possessing in popular form a poetical and philosophical work so dear to India.

There is little else to say which the *Song Celestial* does not explain for itself. The Sanskrit original is written in the *Anushtubh* meter, which cannot be successfully reproduced for Western ears. I have therefore cast it into our flexible blank verse, changing into lyrical measures where the text itself similarly breaks. For the most part, I believe the sense to be faithfully preserved in the following pages; but Schlegel himself had to say: "*In reconditioribus me semper poetae mentem*

recte divinasse affirmare non ausim." *
Those who would read more upon the philosophy of the poem may find an admirable introduction in the volume of Mr. Davies, printed by Messrs. Trübner & Co.

EDWIN ARNOLD, C.S.I.

* "I dare not claim that in more concealed matters I always guess the mind of a poet correctly." *(Publisher's Note)*

CONTENTS

THE SONG CELESTIAL

CHAPTER I

The Distress of Arjuna

Dhritarashtra. Ranged thus for battle on
    the sacred plain—
On Kurukshetra—say, Sanjaya! say
What wrought my people, and the Pandavas?

Sanjaya. When he beheld the host of
    Pandavas,
Raja Duryodhana to Drona drew,
And spake these words: "Ah, Guru! see this
    line,
How vast it is of Pandu fighting-men,
Embattled by the son of Drupada,
Thy scholar in the war! Therein stand ranked
Chiefs like Arjuna, like to Bhima chiefs,
Benders of bows; Virata, Yuyudhan,
Drupada, eminent upon his car,
Dhrishtaket, Chekitan, Kasi's stout lord,
Purujit, Kuntibhoj, and Saivya,
With Yudhamanyu, and Uttamauj,
Subhadra's child; and Draupadi's—all
    famed!

All mounted on their shining chariots!
On our side, too—thou best of Brahmans!
    see
Excellent chiefs, commanders of my line,
Whose names I joy to count: thyself the first,
Then Bhishma, Karna, Kripa fierce in fight,
Vikarna, Aswatthaman; next to these
Strong Saumadatti, with full many more
Valiant and tried, ready this day to die
For me their king, each with his weapon
    grasped,
Each skillful in the field. Weakest—
    meseems—
Our battle shows where Bhishma holds
    command,
And Bhima, fronting him, something too
    strong!
Have care our captains nigh to Bhishma's
    ranks
Prepare what help they may! Now, blow my
    shell!"

    Then, at the signal of the aged king,
With blare to wake the blood, rolling around
Like to a lion's roar, the trumpeter
Blew the great Conch; and, at the noise of it,

Trumpets and drums, cymbals and gongs
    and horns
Burst into sudden clamor; as the blasts
Of loosened tempest, such the tumult
    seemed!
Then might be seen, upon their car of gold
Yoked with white steeds, blowing their
    battle-shells,
Krishna the God, Arjuna at His side:
Krishna, with knotted locks, blew His great
    conch
Carved of the "Giant's bone"; Arjuna blew
Indra's loud gift; Bhima the terrible—
Wolf-bellied Bhima—blew a long reed-
    conch;
And Yudhisthira, Kunti's blameless son,
Winded a mighty shell, "Victory's Voice";
And Nakula blew shrill upon his conch
Named the "Sweet-sounding," Sahadev on
    his
Called "Gem-bedecked," and Kasi's Prince
    on his.
Sikhandi on his car, Dhrishtadyumn,
Virata, Satyaki the Unsubdued,
Drupada, with his sons (O Lord of Earth!),

Long-armed Subhadra's children, all blew
　　loud,
So that the clangor shook their foemen's
　　hearts,
With quaking earth and thundering heav'n.
　　　　　　　　　　　　　Then t'was—
Beholding Dhritarashtra's battle set,
Weapons unsheathing, bows drawn forth,
　　the war
Instant to break—Arjun, whose ensign-
　　badge
Was Hanuman the monkey, spake this thing
To Krishna the Divine, his charioteer:
"Drive, Dauntless One! to yonder open
　　ground
Betwixt the armies; I would see more nigh
These who will fight with us, those we must
　　slay
Today, in war's arbitrament; for, sure,
On bloodshed all are bent who throng this
　　plain,
Obeying Dhritarashtra's sinful son."

　　Thus, by Arjuna prayed (O Bharata!),
Between the hosts that heavenly Charioteer
Drove the bright car, reining its milk-white
　　steeds

Where Bhishma led, and Drona, and their
    Lords.
"See!" spake He to Arjuna, "where they
    stand,
Thy kindred of the Kurus"—and the Prince
Marked on each hand the kinsmen of his
    house,
Grandsires and sires, uncles and brothers
    and sons,
Cousins and sons-in-law and nephews,
    mixed
With friends and honored elders; some
    this side,
Some that side ranged—and, seeing those
    opposed,
Such kith grown enemies, Arjuna's heart
Melted with pity, while he uttered this:

  Arjuna. Krishna! as I behold, come here
    to shed
Their common blood, yon concourse of our
    kin,
My members fail, my tongue dries in my
    mouth,
A shudder thrills my body, and my hair
Bristles with horror; from my weak hand
    slips

Gandiv, the goodly bow; a fever burns
My skin to parching; hardly may I stand;
The life within me seems to swim and faint;
Nothing do I foresee save woe and wail!
It is not good, O Keshav! naught of good
Can spring from mutual slaughter! Lo, I
     hate
Triumph and domination, wealth and ease,
Thus sadly won! *Aho!* what victory
Can bring delight, Govinda! what rich spoils
Could profit; what rule recompense; what
     span
Of life itself seem sweet, bought with such
     blood?
Seeing that these stand here, ready to die,
For whose sake life was fair, and pleasure
     pleased,
And power grew precious: grandsires, sires,
     and sons,
Brothers, and fathers-in-law, and sons-in-
     law,
Elders and friends! Shall I deal death on
     these
Even though they seek to slay us? Not one
     blow,
O Madhusudan! will I strike to gain

The rule of all Three Worlds; then, how
    much less
To seize an earthly kingdom! Killing these
Must breed but anguish, Krishna! If they be
Guilty, we shall grow guilty by their deaths;
Their sins will light on us, if we shall slay
Those sons of Dhritarashtra, and our kin;
What peace could come of that, O Madhava?
For if indeed, blinded by lust and wrath,
These cannot see, or will not see, the sin
Of kingly lines o'erthrown and kinsmen
    slain,
How should not we, who see, shun such a
    crime—
We who perceive the guilt and feel the
    shame—
O Thou Delight of Men, Janardana?
By overthrow of houses perisheth
Their sweet continuous household piety,
And—rites neglected, piety extinct—
Enters impiety upon that home;
Its women grow unwomaned, whence there
    spring
Mad passions, and the mingling-up of castes,
Sending a Hell-ward road that family,

And whoso wrought its doom by wicked
    wrath.
Nay, and the souls of honored ancestors
Fall from their place of peace, being bereft
Of funeral-cakes and the wan death-water.*
So teach our holy hymns. Thus, if we slay
Kinsfolk and friends for love of earthly
    power,
Ahovat! what an evil fault it were!
Better I deem it, if my kinsmen strike,
To face them weaponless, and bare my breast
To shaft and spear, than answer blow with
    blow.

So speaking, in the face of those two hosts,
Arjuna sank upon his chariot-seat,
And let fall bow and arrows, sick at heart.

HERE ENDETH CHAPTER I OF THE
BHAGAVAD-GITA,

Entitled "Arjun-Vishad,"
Or "The Book of the Distress of Arjuna."

* Some repetitionary lines [verses 43,44] are here
omitted.

CHAPTER II

The Book of Doctrines

Sanjaya. Him, filled with such compassion and such grief,
With eyes tear-dimmed, despondent, in stern words
The Driver, Madhusudan, thus addressed:

Krishna. How hath this weakness taken thee? Whence springs
The inglorious trouble, shameful to the brave,
Barring the path of virtue? Nay, Arjun!
Forbid thyself to feebleness! it mars
Thy warrior-name! cast off the coward-fit!
Wake! Be thyself! Arise, Scourge of thy Foes!

Arjuna. How can I, in the battle, shoot with shafts
On Bhishma, or on Drona—O Thou Chief!—
Both worshipful, both honorable men?

11

Better to live on beggar's bread
  With those we love alive,
Than taste their blood in rich feasts
    spread,
  And guiltily survive!

Ah! were it worse—who knows?—
    to be
Victor or vanquished here,
When those confront us angrily
  Whose death leaves living drear?

In pity lost, by doubtings tossed,
  My thoughts—distracted—turn
To Thee, the Guide I reverence most,
  That I may counsel learn:

I know not what would heal the grief
  Burned into soul and sense,
If I were earth's unchallenged chief—
  A god—and these gone thence!

Sanjaya. So spake Arjuna to the Lord of
  Hearts,
And sighing, "I will not fight!" held silence
  then.
To whom, with tender smile (O Bharata!),

While the Prince wept despairing 'twixt
    those hosts,
Krishna made answer in divinest verse:

Krishna. Thou grievest where no grief
    should be! thou speak'st
Words lacking wisdom! for the wise in heart
Mourn not for those that live, nor those that
    die.
Nor I, nor thou, nor any one of these,
Ever was not, nor ever will not be,
Forever and forever afterwards.
All that doth live lives always! To man's
    frame
As there come infancy and youth and age,
So come there raisings-up and layings-down
Of other and of other life-abodes,
Which the wise know, and fear not. This
    that irks—
Thy sense-life, thrilling to the elements—
Bringing thee heat and cold, sorrows and
    joys,
'Tis brief and mutable! Bear with it, Prince!
As the wise bear. The soul which is not
    moved,
The soul that with a strong and constant calm

Takes sorrow and takes joy indifferently,
Lives in the life undying! That which is
Can never cease to be; that which is not
Will not exist. To see this truth of both
Is theirs who part essence from accident,
Substance from shadow. Indestructible,
Learn thou! the Life is, spreading life through
        all;
It cannot anywhere, by any means,
Be anywise diminished, stayed, or changed.
But for these fleeting frames which it informs
With spirit deathless, endless, infinite,
They perish. Let them perish, Prince! and
        fight!
He who shall say, "Lo! I have slain a man!"
He who shall think, "Lo! I am slain!" those
        both
Know naught! Life cannot slay. Life is not
        slain!

    Never the spirit was born; the spirit
            shall cease to be never;
        Never was time it was not; End and
            Beginning are dreams!
    Birthless and deathless and change-
            less remaineth the spirit forever;

Death hath not touched it at all,
    dead though the house of it seems!

Who knoweth it exhaustless, self-sustained,
Immortal, indestructible—shall such
Say, "I have killed a man, or caused to kill"?

    Nay, but as when one layeth
      His worn-out robes away,
    And, taking new ones, sayeth,
      "These will I wear today!"

    So putteth by the spirit
      Lightly its garb of flesh,
    And passeth to inherit
      A residence afresh.

I say to thee weapons reach not the Life,
Flame burns it not, waters cannot o'erwhelm,
Nor dry winds wither it. Impenetrable,
Unentered, unassailed, unharmed,
    untouched,
Immortal, all-arriving, stable, sure,
Invisible, ineffable, by word
And thought uncompassed, ever all itself—
Thus is the Soul declared! How wilt thou,
    then—

Knowing it so—grieve when thou shouldst
    not grieve?
How, if thou hearest that the man new-dead
Is, like the man new-born, still living man—
One same, existent Spirit—wilt thou weep?
The end of birth is death; the end of death
Is birth: this is ordained! and mournest thou,
Chief of the stalwart arm! for what befalls
Which could not otherwise befall? The birth
Of living things comes unperceived; the
    death
Comes unperceived; between them, beings
    perceive:
What is there sorrowful herein, dear Prince?

    Wonderful, wistful, to contemplate!
        Difficult, doubtful, to speak upon!
    Strange and great for tongue to relate,
        Mystical hearing for everyone!
    Nor wotteth man this, what a marvel
        it is,
        When seeing, and saying, and
        hearing are done!

    This Life within all living things, My
        Prince!

Hides beyond harm; scorn thou to suffer,
    then,
For that which cannot suffer. Do thy part!
Be mindful of thy name, and tremble not!
Naught better can betide a martial soul
Than lawful war; happy the warrior
To whom comes joy of battle—comes, as
    now,
Glorious and fair, unsought; opening for him
A gateway unto Heav'n. But, if thou shunn'st
This honorable field—a Kshatriya—
If, knowing thy duty and thy task, thou
    bidd'st
Duty and task go by—that shall be sin!
And those to come shall speak thee infamy
From age to age; but infamy is worse
For men of noble blood to bear than death!
The chiefs upon their battle-chariots
Will deem 'twas fear that drove thee from
    the fray.
Of those who held thee mighty-souled the
    scorn
Thou must abide, while all thine enemies
Will scatter bitter speech of thee, to mock
The valor which thou hadst—what fate
    could fall

More grievously than this? Either—being
    killed—
Thou wilt win Swarga's safety, or—alive
And victor—thou wilt reign an earthly king.
Therefore, arise, thou Son of Kunti! brace
Thine arm for conflict, nerve thy heart to
    meet—
As things alike to thee—pleasure or pain,
Profit or ruin, victory or defeat:
So minded, gird thee to the fight, for so
Thou shalt not sin!

                Thus far I speak to thee
As from the "Sankhya"—unspiritually—
Hear now the deeper teaching of the Yog,
Which holding, understanding, thou shalt
    burst
Thy Karmabandh, the bondage of wrought
    deeds.
Here shall no end be hindered, no hope
    marred,
No loss be feared: faith—yea, a little faith—
Shall save thee from the anguish of thy
    dread.
Here, Glory of the Kurus! shines one rule—
One steadfast rule—while shifting souls
    have laws

Many and hard. Specious, but wrongful deem
The speech of those ill-taught ones who extol
The letter of their Vedas, saying, "This
Is all we have, or need"; being weak at heart
With wants, seekers of Heaven: which comes
  —they say—
As "fruit of good deeds done"; promising
  men
Much profit in new births for works of faith;
In various rites abounding; following
  whereon
Large merit shall accrue towards wealth and
  power;
Albeit, who wealth and power do most desire
Least fixity of soul have such, least hold
On heavenly meditation. Much these teach,
From Veds, concerning the "three qualities";
But thou, be free of the "three qualities,"
Free of the "pairs of opposites,"* and free
From that sad righteousness which calculates;
Self-ruled, Arjuna! simple, satisfied!†
Look! like as when a tank pours water forth
To suit all needs, so do these Brahmans draw

* Technical phrases of Vedic religion.

† The whole of this passage is highly involved and dif-
ficult to render.

Text for all wants from tank of Holy Writ.
But thou, want not! ask not! Find full reward
Of doing right in right! Let right deeds be
Thy motive, not the fruit which comes from
        them.
And live in action! Labor! Make thine acts
Thy piety, casting all self aside,
Contemning gain and merit; equable
In good or evil: equability
Is Yog, is piety!

                        Yet, the right act
Is less, far less, than the right-thinking mind.
Seek refuge in thy soul; have there thy
        heaven!
Scorn them that follow virtue for her gifts!
The mind of pure devotion—even here—
Casts equally aside good deeds and bad,
Passing above them. Unto pure devotion
Devote thyself: with perfect meditation
Comes perfect act, and the right-hearted
        rise—
More certainly because they seek no gain—
Forth from the bands of body, step by step,
To highest seats of bliss. When thy firm soul
Hath shaken off those tangled oracles

Which ignorantly guide, then shall it soar
To high neglect of what's denied or said,
This way or that way, in doctrinal writ.
Troubled no longer by the priestly lore,
Safe shall it live, and sure; steadfastly bent
On meditation. This is Yog—and Peace!

Arjuna. What is his mark who hath that
    steadfast heart,
Confirmed in holy meditation? How
Know we his speech, Kesava? Sits he,
    moves he
Like other men?

Krishna. When one, O Pritha's Son!—
Abandoning desires which shake the mind—
Finds in his soul full comfort for his soul,
He hath attained the Yog—that man is such!
In sorrows not dejected, and in joys
Not overjoyed; dwelling outside the stress
Of passion, fear, and anger; fixed in calms
Of lofty contemplation—such an one
Is Muni, is the Sage, the true Recluse!
He who, to none and nowhere overbound
By ties of flesh, takes evil things and good,
Neither desponding nor exulting, such

Bears wisdom's plainest mark! He who shall
    draw,
As the wise tortoise draws its four feet safe
Under its shield, his five frail senses back
Under the spirit's buckler from the world
Which else assails them—such an one, my
    Prince!
Hath wisdom's mark! Things that solicit
    sense
Hold off from the self-governed; nay, it
    comes,
The appetites of him who lives beyond
Depart, aroused no more. Yet may it
    chance,
O Son of Kunti! that a governed mind
Shall sometime feel the sense-storms sweep,
    and wrest
Strong self-control by the roots. Let him
    regain
His kingdom! let him conquer this, and sit
On Me intent. That man alone is wise
Who keeps the mastery of himself! If one
Ponders on objects of the sense, there springs
Attraction; from attraction grows desire;
Desire flames to fierce passion; passion
    breeds

Recklessness; then the memory—all
    betrayed—
Lets noble purpose go, and saps the mind,
Till purpose, mind, and man are all undone.
But, if one deals with objects of the sense,
Not loving and not hating, making them
Serve his free soul, which rests serenely
    lord,
Lo! such a man comes to tranquillity;
And out of that tranquillity shall rise
The end and healing of his earthly pains,
Since the will governed sets the soul at
    peace.
The soul of the ungoverned is not his,
Nor hath he knowledge of himself; which
    lacked,
How grows serenity? and, wanting that,
Whence shall he hope for happiness?

                    The mind
That gives itself to follow shows of sense
Seeth its helm of wisdom rent away,
And, like a ship in waves of whirlwind,
    drives
To wreck and death. Only with him, great
    Prince!

Whose senses are not swayed by things of
    sense—
Only with him who holds his mastery—
Shows wisdom perfect. What is midnight-
    gloom
To unenlightened souls shines wakeful day
To his clear gaze; what seems as wakeful
    day
Is known for night, thick night of ignorance,
To his true-seeing eyes. Such is the Saint!

And, like the ocean, day by day
        receiving
    Floods from all lands, which never
        overflows—
Its boundary-line not leaping, and not
        leaving,
    Fed by the rivers, but unswelled by
        those—

So is the perfect one! To his soul's
        ocean
    The world of sense pours streams of
        witchery;
They leave him as they find, without
        commotion,

Taking their tribute, but remaining
   sea.

Yea! whoso, shaking off the yoke of flesh,
Lives lord, not servant, of his lusts—set free
From pride, from passion, from the sin of
   "Self"—
Toucheth tranquillity! O Pritha's Son!
That is the state of Brahm! There rests no
   dread
When that last step is reached! Live where
   he will,
Die when he may, such passeth from all
   'plaining,
To blest Nirvana, with the Gods, attaining.

HERE ENDETH CHAPTER II OF THE
   BHAGAVAD-GITA,

Entitled "Sankhya-Yog,"
Or "The Book of Doctrines."

CHAPTER III

Virtue in Work

Arjuna. Thou whom all mortals praise,
  Janardana!
If meditation be a nobler thing
Than action, wherefore then, great Kesava!
Dost thou impel me to this dreadful fight?
Now am I by Thy doubtful speech disturbed!
Tell me one thing, and tell me certainly:
By what road shall I find the better end?

Krishna. I told thee, blameless Lord! there
  be two paths
Shown to this world, two schools of wisdom.
  First
The Sankhya's, which doth save in way of
  works
Prescribed by reason; next, the Yog, which
  bids
Attain by meditation, spiritually:
Yet these are one! No man shall 'scape from
  act
By shunning action; nay, and none shall
  come

27

By mere renouncements unto perfectness.
Nay, and no jot of time, at any time,
Rests any actionless; his nature's law
Compels him, even unwilling, into act;
[For thought is act in fancy]. He who sits
Suppressing all the instruments of flesh,
Yet in his idle heart thinking on them,
Plays the inept and guilty hypocrite;
But he who, with strong body serving mind,
Gives up his mortal powers to worthy work,
Not seeking gain, Arjuna! such an one
Is honorable. Do thine allotted task!
Work is more excellent than idleness;
The body's life proceeds not, lacking work.
There is a task of holiness to do—
Unlike world-binding toil—which bindeth
        not
The faithful soul; such earthly duty do
Free from desire, and thou shalt well perform
Thy heavenly purpose. Spake Prajapati—
In the beginning, when all men were made,
And, with mankind, the sacrifice—"Do this!
Work! sacrifice! Increase and multiply
With sacrifice! This shall be Kamadhuk,
Your 'Cow of Plenty,' giving back her milk
Of all abundance. Worship the gods thereby;

The gods shall yield thee grace. Those meats
    ye crave
The gods will grant to Labor, when it pays
Tithes in the altar-flame. But if one eats
Fruits of the earth, rendering to kindly Heaven
No gift of toil, that thief steals from his
    world."

    Who eat of food after their sacrifice
Are quit of fault, but they that spread a feast
All for themselves eat sin and drink of sin.
By food the living live; food comes of rain,
And rain comes by the pious sacrifice,
And sacrifice is paid with tithes of toil;
Thus action is of Brahma, who is One,
The Only, All-pervading, at all times
Present in sacrifice. He that abstains
To help the rolling wheels of this great
    world,
Glutting his idle sense, lives a lost life,
Shameful and vain. Existing for himself,
Self-concentrated, serving self alone,
No part hath he in aught; nothing achieved,
Naught wrought or unwrought toucheth
    him; no hope

Of help for all the living things of earth
Depends from him.* Therefore, thy task
    prescribed
With spirit unattached gladly perform,
Since in performance of plain duty man
Mounts to his highest bliss. By works alone
Janak and ancient saints reached
    blessedness!
Moreover, for the upholding of thy kind,
Action thou should'st embrace. What the
    wise choose
The unwise people take; what best men do
The multitude will follow. Look on Me,
Thou Son of Pritha! in the three wide worlds
I am not bound to any toil—no height
Awaits to scale, no gift remains to gain—
Yet I act here! and, if I acted not—
Earnest and watchful—those that look to Me
For guidance, sinking back to sloth again
Because I slumbered, would decline from
    good,
And I should break earth's order and commit
Her offspring unto ruin, Bharata!
Even as the unknowing toil, wedded to sense,

* I am doubtful of accuracy here.

So let the enlightened toil, sense-freed, but
    set
To bring the world deliverance, and its bliss;
Not sowing in those simple, busy hearts
Seed of despair. Yea! let each play his part
In all he finds to do, with unyoked soul.
All things are everywhere by Nature wrought
In interaction of the qualities.
The fool, cheated by self, thinks, "This I did"
And "That I wrought"; but—ah, thou strong-
    armed Prince!—
A better-lessoned mind, knowing the play
Of visible things within the world of sense,
And how the qualities must qualify,
Standeth aloof even from his acts.

      Th' untaught
Live mixed with them, knowing not Nature's
    way,
Of highest aims unwitting, slow and dull.
Those make thou not to stumble, having the
    light;
But all thy dues discharging, for My sake,
With meditation centered inwardly—
Seeking no profit, satisfied, serene,
Heedless of issue—fight! They who shall
    keep

My ordinance thus, the wise and willing
    hearts,
Have quittance from all issue of their acts;
But those who disregard My ordinance,
Thinking they know, know naught, and fall
    to loss,
Confused and foolish. 'Sooth, the instructed
    one
Doth of his kind, following what fits him
    most;
And lower creatures of their kind, in vain
Contending 'gainst the law. Needs must it be
The objects of the sense will stir the sense
To like and dislike, yet th' enlightened man
Yields not to these, knowing them enemies.
Finally, this is better, that one do
His own task as he may, even though he fail,
Than take tasks not his own, though they
    seem good.
To die performing duty is no ill;
But who seeks other roads shall wander still.

    Arjuna. Yet tell me, Teacher! by what
    force doth man
Go to his ill, unwilling—as if one
Pushed him that evil path?

Krishna. Kama it is!
Passion it is! born of the Darknesses,
Which pusheth him. Mighty of appetite,
Sinful, and strong is this!—man's enemy!
As smoke blots the white fire, as clinging rust
Mars the bright mirror, as the womb
    surrounds
The babe unborn—so is the world of things
Foiled, soiled, enclosed in this desire of
    flesh.
The wise fall, caught in it; the unresting foe
It is of wisdom, wearing countless forms,
Fair but deceitful, subtle as a flame.
Sense, mind, and reason—these, O Kunti's
    Son!
Are booty for it; in its play with these
It maddens man, beguiling, blinding him.
Therefore, thou noblest child of Bharata!
Govern thy heart! Constrain th' entangled
    sense!
Resist the false, soft sinfulness which saps
Knowledge and judgment! Yea, the world is
    strong,
But what discerns it stronger, and the mind
Strongest; and high o'er all the ruling Soul.

Wherefore, perceiving Him who reigns
    supreme,
Put forth full force of Soul in thy own soul!
Fight! vanquish foes and doubts, dear Hero!
    slay
What haunts thee in fond shapes, and would
    betray!

HERE ENDETH CHAPTER III OF THE
    BHAGAVAD-GITA,

Entitled "Karma-Yog,"
Or "The Book of Virtue in Work."

CHAPTER IV

The Religion of Knowledge

Krishna. This deathless Yoga, this deep
  union,
I taught Vivaswata,* the Lord of Light;
Vivaswata to Manu gave it; he
To Ikshwaku; so passed it down the line
Of all My royal Rishis. Then, with years,
The truth grew dim and perished, noble
  Prince!
Now once again to thee it is declared—
This ancient lore, this mystery supreme—
Seeing I find thee votary and friend.

Arjuna. Thy birth, dear Lord, was in these
  later days,
And bright Vivaswata's preceded time!
How shall I comprehend this thing thou
  sayest,
"From the beginning it was I who taught?"

Krishna. Manifold the renewals of My
  birth

* A name of the sun.

Have been, Arjuna! and of thy births, too!
But Mine I know, and thine thou knowest
    not,
O Slayer of thy Foes! Albeit I be
Unborn, undying, indestructible,
The Lord of all things living; not the less—
By Maya, by My magic which I stamp
On floating Nature-forms, the primal vast—
I come, and go, and come. When
    Righteousness
Declines, O Bharata! when Wickedness
Is strong, I rise, from age to age, and take
Visible shape, and move a man with men,
Succoring the good, thrusting the evil back,
And setting Virtue on her seat again.
Who knows the truth touching My births on
    earth
And My divine work, when he quits the
    flesh
Puts on its load no more, falls no more down
To earthly birth: to Me he comes, dear Prince!

Many there be who come! from fear set
    free,
From anger, from desire; keeping their hearts
Fixed upon Me—My Faithful—purified

By sacred flame of Knowledge. Such as these
Mix with My being. Whoso worship Me,
Them I exalt; but all men everywhere
Shall fall into My path; albeit, those souls
Which seek reward for works, make sacrifice
Now, to the lower gods. I say to thee
Here have they their reward. But I am He
Made the Four Castes, and portioned them
    a place
After their qualities and gifts. Yea, I
Created, the Reposeful; I that live
Immortally, made all those mortal births:
For works soil not My essence, being works
Wrought uninvolved.* Who knows Me
    acting thus
Unchained by action, action binds not him;
And, so perceiving, all those saints of old
Worked, seeking for deliverance. Work thou
As, in the days gone by, thy fathers did.

   Thou sayst, perplexed—it hath been
    asked before
By singers and by sages—"What is act,
And what inaction?" I will teach thee this,

---

* Without desire of fruit.

And, knowing, thou shalt learn which work
    doth save.
Needs must one rightly meditate those three:
Doing, not doing, and undoing. Here
Thorny and dark the path is! He who sees
How action may be rest, rest action—he
Is wisest 'mid his kind; he hath the truth!
He doeth well, acting or resting. Freed
In all his works from prickings of desire,
Burned clean in act by the white fire of
    truth—
The wise call that man wise; and such an
    one,
Renouncing fruit of deeds, always content,
Always self-satisfying, if he works,
Doth nothing that shall stain his separate
    soul,
Which—quit of fear and hope, subduing
    self,
Rejecting outward impulse, yielding up
To body's need nothing save body—dwells
Sinless amid all sin, with equal calm
Taking what may befall, by grief unmoved,
Unmoved by joy, unenvyingly; the same
In good and evil fortunes; nowise bound
By bond of deeds. Nay, but of such an one,

Whose crave is gone, whose soul is liberate,
Whose heart is set on truth—of such an
    one,

What work he does is work of sacrifice,
Which passeth purely into ash and smoke
Consumed upon the altar! All's then God!
The sacrifice is Brahm, the ghee and grain
Are Brahm, the fire is Brahm, the flesh it
    eats

Is Brahm; and unto Brahm attaineth he
Who, in such office, meditates on Brahm.
Some votaries there be who serve the gods
With flesh and altar-smoke; but other some
Who, lighting subtler fires, make purer rite
With will of worship. Of the which be they
Who, in white flame of continence, consume
Joys of the sense, delights of eye and ear,
Forgoing tender speech and sound of song:
And they who, kindling fires with torch of
    Truth,

Burn on a hidden altar-stone the bliss
Of youth and love, renouncing happiness:
And they who lay for offering there their
    wealth,

Their penance, meditation, piety,

Their steadfast reading of the scrolls, their
    lore
Painfully gained with long austerities:
And they who, making silent sacrifice,
Draw in their breath to feed the flame of
    thought,
And breathe it forth to waft the heart on
    high,
Governing the ventage of each entering air
Lest one sigh pass which helpeth not the
    soul:
And they who, day by day denying needs,
Lay life itself upon the altar-flame,
Burning the body wan. Lo! all these keep
The rite of offering, as if they slew
Victims; and all thereby efface much sin.
Yea! and who feed on the immortal food
Left of such sacrifice, to Brahma pass,
To The Unending. But for him that makes
No sacrifice, he hath nor part nor lot
Even in the present world. How should he
    share
Another, O thou Glory of thy Line?

    In sight of Brahma all these offerings
Are spread and are accepted! Comprehend

That all proceed by act; for knowing this,
Thou shalt be quit of doubt. The sacrifice
Which Knowledge pays is better than great
　　gifts
Offered by wealth, since gifts' worth, O My
　　Prince!
Lies in the mind which gives, the will that
　　serves;
And these are gained by reverence, by strong
　　search,
By humble heed of those who see the Truth
And teach it. Knowing Truth, thy heart no
　　more
Will ache with error, for the Truth shall show
All things subdued to thee, as thou to Me.
Moreover, Son of Pandu! wert thou worst
Of all wrong-doers, this fair ship of Truth
Should bear thee safe and dry across the sea
Of thy transgressions. As the kindled flame
Feeds on the fuel till it sinks to ash,
So unto ash, Arjuna! unto naught
The flame of Knowledge wastes works' dross
　　away!
There is no purifier like thereto
In all this world, and he who seeketh it

Shall find it—being grown perfect—in
    himself.
Believing, he receives it when the soul
Masters itself, and cleaves to Truth, and
    comes—
Possessing knowledge—to the higher peace,
The uttermost repose. But those untaught,
And those without full faith, and those who
    fear
Are shent; no peace is here or other where—
No hope, nor happiness for whoso doubts.
He that, being self-contained, hath
    vanquished doubt,
Disparting self from service, soul from
    works,
Enlightened and emancipate, My Prince!
Works fetter him no more! Cut then atwain
With sword of wisdom, Son of Bharata!
This doubt that binds thy heart-beats! cleave
    the bond
Born of thy ignorance! Be bold and wise!
Give thyself to the field with Me! Arise!

HERE ENDETH CHAPTER IV OF THE
BHAGAVAD-GITA,
Entitled "Jnana Yog,"
Or "The Book of the Religion of Knowledge."

CHAPTER V

Religion by Renouncing
Fruit of Works

Arjuna. Yet, Krishna! at the one time
    Thou dost laud
Surcease of works, and at another time,
Service through work. Of these twain plainly
    tell
Which is the better way?

Krishna.   To cease from works
Is well, and to do works in holiness
Is well; and both conduct to bliss supreme;
But of these twain the better way is his
Who working piously refraineth not.

That is the true Renouncer, firm and fixed,
Who—seeking naught, rejecting naught—
    dwells proof
Against the "opposites."* O valiant Prince!
In doing, such breaks lightly from all deed—

* That is "joy and sorrow, success and failure, heat
and cold," etc.

'Tis the new scholar talks as they were two,
This Sankhya and this Yoga—wise men
    know
Who husbands one plucks golden fruit of
    both!
The region of high rest which Sankhyans
    reach
Yogins attain. Who sees these twain as one
Sees with clear eyes! Yet such abstraction,
    Chief!
Is hard to win without much holiness.
Whoso is fixed in holiness, self-ruled,
Pure-hearted, lord of senses and of self,
Lost in the common life of all which lives—
A "Yogayukt"—he is a Saint who wends
Straightway to Brahm. Such an one is not
    touched
By taint of deeds. "Naught of myself I do!"
Thus will he think, who holds the truth of
    truths—
In seeing, hearing, touching, smelling; when
He eats, or goes, or breathes; slumbers or
    talks,
Holds fast or loosens, opens his eyes or shuts;
Always assured "This is the sense-world
    plays

With senses." He that acts in thought of
    Brahm,
Detaching end from act, with act content,
The world of sense can no more stain his soul
Than waters mar th' enameled lotus-leaf.
With life, with heart, with mind—nay,
    with the help
Of all five senses—letting selfhood go,
Yogins toil ever towards their souls' release.
Such votaries, renouncing fruit of deeds,
Gain endless peace; the unvowed, the
    passion-bound,
Seeking a fruit from works, are fastened down.
The embodied sage, withdrawn within his
    soul,
At every act sits godlike in "the town
Which hath nine gateways,"* neither doing
    aught
Nor causing any deed. This world's Lord
    makes
Neither the work, nor passion for the work,
Nor lust for fruit of work; the man's own self
Pushes to these! The Master of this World
Takes on himself the good or evil deeds

* *i.e.*, the body.

Of no man—dwelling beyond! Mankind
    errs here
By folly, darkening knowledge. But, for
    whom
That darkness of the soul is chased by light,
Splendid and clear shines manifest the Truth
As if a Sun of Wisdom sprang to shed
Its beams of dawn. Him meditating still,
Him seeking, with Him blended, stayed on
    Him,
The souls illuminated take that road
Which hath no turning back—their sins
    flung off
By strength of faith. [Who will may have this
    Light;
Who hath it sees.] To him who wisely sees,
The Brahman with his scrolls and sanctities,
The cow, the elephant, the unclean dog,
The Outcast gorging dog's meat, are all one.

    The world is overcome—aye! even here!
By such as fix their faith on Unity.
The sinless Brahma dwells in Unity,
And they in Brahma. Be not over-glad
Attaining joy, and be not over-sad

Encountering grief; but stayed on Brahma,
   still
Constant let each abide! The sage whose
   soul
Holds off from outer contacts, in himself
Finds bliss; to Brahma joined by piety,
His spirit tastes eternal peace. The joys
Springing from sense-life are but quickening
   wombs
Which breed sure griefs: those joys begin
   and end!
The wise mind takes no pleasure, Kunti's
   Son!
In such as those! But if a man shall learn,
Even while he lives and bears his body's
   chain,
To master lust and anger, he is blest!
He is the *Yukta*; he hath happiness,
Contentment, light, within: his life is merged
In Brahma's life; he doth Nirvana touch!
Thus go the Rishis unto rest, who dwell
With sins effaced, with doubts at end, with
   hearts
Governed and calm. Glad in all good they
   live,
Nigh to the peace of God; and all those live

Who pass their days exempt from greed and
    wrath,
Subduing self and senses, knowing the Soul!

  The Saint who shuts outside his placid
    soul
All touch of sense, letting no contact through;
Whose quiet eyes gaze straight from fixèd
    brows,
Whose outward breath and inward breath
    are drawn
Equal and slow through nostrils still and
    close;
That one—with organs, heart, and mind
    constrained,
Bent on deliverance, having put away
Passion, and fear, and rage—hath, even
    now,
Obtained deliverance, ever and ever freed.
Yea! for he knows Me Who am He that heeds
The sacrifice and worship, God revealed;
And He who heeds not, being Lord of Worlds,
Lover of all that lives, God unrevealed,
Wherein who will shall find surety and
    shield!

HERE ENDS CHAPTER V OF THE
BHAGAVAD-GITA,

Entitled "Karmasanyasayog,"
Or "The Book of Religion by Renouncing
Fruit of Works."

CHAPTER VI

Religion by Self-Restraint

Krishna. Therefore, who doeth work right-
ful to do,
Not seeking gain from work, that man, O
Prince!
Is Sannyasi and Yogi—both in one—
And he is neither who lights not the flame
Of sacrifice, nor setteth hand to task.

Regard as true Renouncer him that makes
Worship by work, for who renounceth not
Works not as Yogin. So is that well said:
"By works the votary doth rise to saint,
And saintship is the ceasing from all works";
Because the perfect Yogin acts—but acts
Unmoved by passions and unbound by
deeds,
Setting result aside.

Let each man raise
The Self by Soul, not trample down his
Self,

Since Soul that is Self's friend may grow
    Self's foe.
Soul is Self's friend when Self doth rule o'er
    Self,
But Self turns enemy if Soul's own self
Hates Self as not itself.*

                 The sovereign soul
Of him who lives self-governed and at peace
Is centered in itself, taking alike
Pleasure and pain; heat, cold; glory and
    shame.
He is the Yogi, he is *Yukta*, glad
With joy of light and truth—dwelling apart
Upon a peak, with senses subjugate
Whereto the clod, the rock, the glistering
    gold
Show all as one. By this sign is he known
Being of equal grace to comrades, friends,
Chance-comers, strangers, lovers, enemies,
Aliens and kinsmen—loving all alike,
Evil or good.

              Sequestered should he sit,
Steadfastly meditating, solitary,

* The Sanskrit has this play on the double meaning
of *Atman*.

His thoughts controlled, his passions laid
    away,
Quit of belongings. In a fair, still spot
Having his fixed abode—not too much
    raised,
Nor yet too low—let him abide, his goods
A cloth, a deerskin, and the Kusa-grass.
There, setting hard his mind upon The One,
Restraining heart and senses, silent, calm,
Let him accomplish Yoga, and achieve
Pureness of soul, holding immovable
Body and neck and head, his gaze absorbed
Upon his nose-end,* rapt from all around,
Tranquil in spirit, free of fear, intent
Upon his Brahmacharya vow, devout,
Musing on Me, lost in the thought of Me.
That Yogin, so devoted, so controlled,
Comes to the peace beyond—My peace, the
    peace
Of high Nirvana!

               But for earthly needs
Religion is not his who too much fasts
Or too much feasts, nor his who sleeps away
An idle mind, nor his who wears to waste

* So in original.

His strength in vigils. Nay, Arjuna! call
That the true piety which most removes
Earth-aches and ills, where one is moderate
In eating and in resting and in sport—
Measured in wish and act—sleeping betimes,
Waking betimes for duty.
                            When the man,
So living, centers on his soul the thought
Straitly restrained—untouched internally
By stress of sense—then is he *Yukta*. See!
Steadfast a lamp burns sheltered from the
    wind—
Such is the likeness of the Yogi's mind
Shut from sense-storms and burning bright
    to Heaven.
When mind broods placid, soothed with
    holy wont;
When Self contemplates self, and in itself
Hath comfort; when it knows the nameless
    joy
Beyond all scope of sense, revealed to soul,
Only to soul! and, knowing, wavers not,
True to the farther Truth; when, holding this,
It deems no other treasure comparable,
But, harbored there, cannot be stirred or
    shook

By any gravest grief—call that state "peace,"
That happy severance Yoga; call that man
The perfect Yogin!

          Steadfastly the will
Must toil thereto, till efforts end in ease,
And thought has passed from thinking.
    Shaking off
All longings bred by dreams of fame and
    gain,
Shutting the doorways of the senses close
With watchful ward; so, step by step, it
    comes
To gift of peace assured and heart assuaged,
When the mind dwells self-wrapped, and the
    soul broods
Cumberless. But, as often as the heart
Breaks—wild and wavering—from control,
    so oft
Let him re-curb it, let him rein it back
To the soul's governance; for perfect bliss
Grows only in the bosom tranquilized,
The spirit passionless, purged from
    offence,
Vowed to the Infinite. He who thus vows
His soul to the Supreme Soul, quitting sin,

Passes unhindered to the endless bliss
Of unity with Brahma. He so vowed,
So blended, sees the Life-Soul resident
In all things living, and all living things
In that Life-Soul contained. And whoso thus
Discerneth Me in all, and all in Me,
I never let him go, nor looseneth he
Hold upon Me; but, dwell he where he may,
Whate'er his life, in Me he dwells and lives,
Because he knows and worships Me, Who
        dwell
In all which lives, and cleaves to Me in all.
Arjuna! if a man sees everywhere—
Taught by his own similitude—one Life,
One Essence in the Evil and the Good,
Hold him a Yogi, yea! well-perfected!

  Arjuna. Slayer of Madhu! yet again, this
        Yog,
This Peace, derived from equanimity,
Made known by Thee—I see no fixity
Therein, no rest, because the heart of men
Is unfixed, Krishna! rash, tumultuous,
Willful and strong. It were all one, I think,
To hold the wayward wind, as tame man's
        heart.

Krishna. Hero long-armed! beyond denial,
   hard
Man's heart is to restrain, and wavering;
Yet may it grow restrained by habit, Prince!
By wont of self-command. This Yog, I say,
Cometh not lightly to th' ungoverned ones;
But he who will be master of himself
Shall win it, if he stoutly strive thereto.

Arjuna. And what road goeth he who,
   having faith,
Fails, Krishna! in the striving—falling back
From holiness, missing the perfect rule?
Is he not lost, straying from Brahma's light,
Like the vain cloud, which floats 'twixt earth
   and heaven
When lightning splits it, and it vanisheth?
Fain would I hear Thee answer me herein,
Since, Krishna! none save Thou can clear
   the doubt.

Krishna. He is not lost, thou Son of Pritha!
   No!
Nor earth, nor heaven is forfeit, even for him,
Because no heart that holds one right desire
Treadeth the road of loss! He who should
   fail,

Desiring righteousness, cometh at death
Unto the Region of the Just; dwells there
Measureless years, and being born anew,
Beginneth life again in some fair home
Amid the mild and happy. It may chance
He doth descend into a Yogin house
On Virtue's breast, but that is rare! Such birth
Is hard to be obtained on this earth, Chief!
So hath he back again what heights of heart
He did achieve, and so he strives anew
To perfectness, with better hope, dear Prince!
For by the old desire he is drawn on
Unwittingly; and only to desire
The purity of Yog is to pass
Beyond the *Sabdabrahm*, the spoken Ved.
But, being Yogi, striving strong and long,
Purged from transgressions, perfected by
          births
Following on births, he plants his feet at last
Upon the farther path. Such an one ranks
Above ascetics, higher than the wise,
Beyond achievers of vast deeds! Be thou
Yogi, Arjuna! And of such believe,
Truest and best is he who worships Me
With inmost soul, stayed on My Mystery!

HERE ENDETH CHAPTER VI OF THE
BHAGAVAD-GITA,

Entitled *"Atmasanyamayog,"*
Or *"The Book of Religion by Self-Restraint."*

CHAPTER VII

Religion by Discernment

Krishna. Learn now, dear Prince! how, if
  thy soul be set
Ever on Me—still exercising Yog,
Still making Me thy Refuge—thou shalt
  come
Most surely unto perfect hold of Me.
I will declare to thee that utmost lore,
Whole and particular, which, when thou
  knowest,
Leaveth no more to know here in this world.

Of many thousand mortals, one,
  perchance,
Striveth for Truth; and of those few that
  strive—
Nay, and rise high—one only—here and
  there—
Knoweth Me, as I am, the very Truth.

Earth, water, flame, air, ether, life, and
  mind,

And individuality—those eight
Make up the showing of Me, Manifest.

   These be My lower Nature; learn the higher,
Whereby, thou Valiant One! this Universe
Is, by its principle of life, produced;
Whereby the worlds of visible things are
    born
As from a *Yoni*. Know! I am that womb—
I make and I unmake this Universe—
Than Me there is no other Master, Prince!
No other Maker! All these hang on Me
As hangs a row of pearls upon its string.
I am the fresh taste of the water; I
The silver of the moon, the gold o' the sun,
The word of worship in the Veds, the thrill
That passeth in the ether, and the strength
Of man's shed seed. I am the good sweet
    smell
Of the moistened earth, I am the fire's red
    light,
The vital air moving in all which moves,
The holiness of hallowed souls, the root
Undying, whence hath sprung whatever is;
The wisdom of the wise, the intellect
Of the informed, the greatness of the great,

The splendor of the splendid. Kunti's Son!
These am I, free from passion and desire;
Yet am I right desire in all who yearn,
Chief of the Bharatas! for all those moods,
Soothfast, or passionate, or ignorant,
Which Nature frames, deduce from Me;
 but all
Are merged in Me—not I in them! The
 world—
Deceived by those three qualities of being—
Wotteth not Me Who am outside them all,
Above them all, Eternal! Hard it is
To pierce that veil divine of various shows
Which hideth Me; yet they who worship Me
Pierce it and pass beyond.
       I am not known
To evil-doers, nor to foolish ones,
Nor to the base and churlish; nor to those
Whose mind is cheated by the show of things,
Nor those that take the way of Asuras.*

 Four sorts of mortals know Me: he who
  weeps,
Arjuna! and the man who yearns to know;
And he who toils to help; and he who sits

* Beings of low and devilish nature.

Certain of Me, enlightened.

> Of these four,

O Prince of India! highest, nearest, best
That last is, the devout soul, wise, intent
Upon "The One." Dear, above all, am I
To him; and he is dearest unto Me!
All four are good, and seek Me; but Mine
> own,
The true of heart, the faithful—stayed on
> Me,
Taking Me as their utmost blessedness,
They are not "Mine," but I—even I Myself!
At end of many births to Me they come!
Yet hard the wise Mahatma is to find,
That man who sayeth, "All is Vasudev!"*

There be those, too, whose knowledge,
> turned aside
By this desire or that, gives them to serve
Some lower gods, with various rites,
> constrained
By that which mouldeth them. Unto all
> such—
Worship what shrine they will, what shapes,
> in faith—

---

* Krishna.

'Tis I who give them faith! I am content!
The heart thus asking favor from its God,
Darkened but ardent, hath the end it craves,
The lesser blessing—but 'tis I who give!
Yet soon is withered what small fruit they
    reap:
Those men of little minds, who worship so,
Go where they worship, passing with their
    gods.
But Mine come unto Me! Blind are the eyes
Which deem th' Unmanifested manifest,
Not comprehending Me in My true Self!
Imperishable, viewless, undeclared,
Hidden behind My magic veil of shows,
I am not seen by all; I am not known—
Unborn and changeless—to the idle world.
But I, Arjuna! know all things which were,
And all which are, and all which are to be,
Albeit not one among them knoweth Me!

  By passion for the "pairs of opposites,"
By those twain snares of Like and Dislike,
    Prince!
All creatures live bewildered, save some few
Who, quit of sins, holy in act, informed,

Freed from the "opposites," and fixed in
    faith,
Cleave unto Me.

               Who cleave, who seek in Me
Refuge from birth* and death, those have the
    Truth!
Those know Me BRAHMA; know Me Soul of
    Souls,
The ADHYATMAN; know KARMA, My work;
Know I am ADHIBHUTA, Lord of Life,
And ADHIDAIVA, Lord of all the Gods,
And ADHIYAJNA, Lord of Sacrifice;
Worship Me well, with hearts of love and
    faith,
And find and hold Me in the hour of death.

HERE ENDETH CHAPTER VII OF THE
BHAGAVAD-GITA,

Entitled "Vijnanayog,"
Or "The Book of Religion by Discernment."

---

* I read here *janma*, "birth"; not *jara*, "age."

Wherefrom who comprehends My Reign of
    mystic Majesty—
That truth of truths—is thenceforth linked
    in faultless faith to Me:

Yea! knowing Me the source of all, by Me
    all creatures wrought,
The wise in spirit cleave to Me, into My
    Being brought;

Hearts fixed on Me; breaths breathed to Me;
    praising Me, each to each,
So have they happiness and peace, with
    pious thought and speech;

And unto these—thus serving well, thus
    loving ceaselessly—
I give a mind of perfect mood, whereby they
    draw to Me;

And all for love of them, within their
    darkened souls I dwell,
And with bright rays of wisdom's lamp,
    their ignorance dispel.

    Arjuna. Yes! Thou art Parabrahm! The
    High Abode!
The Great Purification! Thou art God

Eternal, All-creating, Holy, First,
Without beginning! Lord of Lords and Gods!
Declared by all the Saints—by Narada,
Vyasa, Asita, and Devalas—
And here Thyself declaring unto me!
What Thou hast said now know I to be truth,
O Kesava! that neither gods nor men
Nor demons comprehend Thy mystery
Made manifest, Divinest! Thou Thyself
Thyself alone dost know, Maker Supreme!
Master of all the living! Lord of Gods!
King of the Universe! To Thee alone
Belongs to tell the heavenly excellence
Of those perfections wherewith Thou dost
        fill
These worlds of Thine—Pervading,
        Immanent!
How shall I learn, Supremest Mystery!
To know Thee, though I muse continually?
Under what form of Thine unnumbered
        forms
Mayest Thou be grasped? Ah! yet again
        recount,
Clear and complete, Thy great appearances,
The secrets of Thy Majesty and Might,
Thou High Delight of Men! Never enough

Can mine ears drink the Amrit* of such
    words!

  Krishna. *Hanta!* So be it! Kuru Prince! I
    will to thee unfold
Some portions of My Majesty, whose powers
    are manifold!

I am the Spirit seated deep in every creature's
    heart;
From Me they come; by Me they live; at My
    word they depart!

Vishnu of the Adityas I am, those Lords of
    Light;
Maritchi of the Maruts, the Kings of Storm
    and Blight;

By day I gleam, the golden Sun of burning
    cloudless Noon;
By Night, amid the asterisms I glide, the
    dappled Moon!

Of Vedas I am Sama-Ved, of gods in Indra's
    Heaven
Vasava; of the faculties to living beings given

The mind which apprehends and thinks; of
    Rudras Sankara;

* The nectar of Immortality.

Of Yakshas and of Rakshasas, Vittesh; and
    Pavaka

Of Vasus, and of mountain-peaks Meru;
    Vrihaspati
Know Me 'mid planetary Powers; 'mid
    Warriors heavenly

Skanda; of all the water-floods the Sea which
    drinketh each,
And Bhrigu of the holy Saints, and OM of
    sacred speech;

Of prayers the prayer ye whisper;* of hills
    Himala's snow,
And Aswattha, the fig-tree, of all the trees
    that grow;

Of the Devarshis, Narada; and Chitrarath
    of them
That sing in Heaven, and Kapila of Munis,
    and the gem

Of flying steeds, Uchchaisravas, from Amrit-
    wave which burst;
Of elephants Airavata; of males the Best and
    First;

* Called "The Jap."

Of weapons Heav'n's hot thunderbolt; of
    cows white Kamadhuk,

From whose great milky udder-teats all
    heart's desires are strook;

Vasuki of the serpent-tribes, round Mandara
    entwined;

And thousand-fanged Ananta, on whose
    broad coils reclined

Leans Vishnu; and of water-things Varuna;
    Aryam

Of Pitris, and of those that judge, Yama the
    Judge I am;

Of Daityas dread Prahlada; of what metes
    days and years,

Time's self I am; of woodland-beasts—
    buffaloes, deers, and bears—

The lordly-painted tiger; of birds the vast
    Garud,

The whirlwind 'mid the winds; 'mid chiefs
    Rama with blood imbrued,

Makar 'mid fishes of the sea, and Ganges
    'mid the streams;

Yea! First, and Last, and Center of all which
    is or seems

I am, Arjuna! Wisdom Supreme of what is
    wise,
Words on the uttering lips I am, and eyesight
    of the eyes,
And "A" of written characters, Dwandwa*
    of knitted speech,
And Endless Life, and boundless Love,
    whose power sustaineth each;
And bitter Death which seizes all, and
    joyous sudden Birth,
Which brings to light all beings that are to be
    on earth;
And of the viewless virtues, Fame, Fortune,
    Song am I,
And Memory, and Patience; and Craft, and
    Constancy:
Of Vedic hymns the Vrihatsam, of meters
    Gayatri,
Of months the Margasirsha, of all the seasons
    three
The flower-wreathed Spring; in dicer's-play
    the conquering Double-Eight;

* The compound form of Sanskrit words.

The splendor of the splendid, and the
    greatness of the great,

Victory I am, and Action! and the goodness
    of the good,

And Vasudev of Vrishni's race, and of this
    Pandu brood

Thyself!—Yea, My Arjuna! thyself; for thou
    art Mine!

Of poets Usana, of saints Vyasa, sage divine;

The policy of conquerors, the potency of
    kings,

The great unbroken silence in learning's
    secret things;

The lore of all the learnèd, the seed of all
    which springs.

Living or lifeless, still or stirred, whatever
    beings be,

None of them is in all the worlds, but it
    exists by Me!

Nor tongue can tell, Arjuna! nor end of telling
    come

Of these My boundless glories, whereof I
    teach thee some;

For wheresoe'er is wondrous work, and
  majesty, and might,
From Me hath all proceeded. Receive thou
  this aright!

Yet how shouldst thou receive, O Prince!
  the vastness of this word?
I, who am all, and made it all, abide its
  separate Lord!

HERE ENDETH CHAPTER X OF THE
BHAGAVAD-GITA,

Entitled "Vibhuti Yog,"
*Or "The Book of Religion by the Heavenly
Perfections."*

CHAPTER XI

The Manifesting of the One and Manifold

Arjuna. This, for my soul's peace, have I
  heard from Thee,
The unfolding of the Mystery Supreme
Named Adhyatman—comprehending
  which,
My darkness is dispelled; for now I know,
O Lotus-eyed!* whence is the birth of men,
And whence their death, and what the
  majesties
Of Thine immortal rule. Fain would I see,
As Thou Thyself declar'st it, Sovereign Lord!
The likeness of that glory of Thy Form
Wholly revealed. O Thou Divinest One!
If this can be, if I may bear the sight,
Make Thyself visible, Lord of all prayers!
Show me Thy very self, the Eternal God!

Krishna. Gaze then, thou Son of Pritha!
  I manifest for thee

* "Kamalapatraksha."

Those hundred thousand thousand shapes
    that clothe My Mystery:

I show thee all My semblances—infinite,
    rich, divine—

My changeful hues, My countless forms.
    See! in this face of Mine,

Adityas, Vasus, Rudras, Aswins, and
    Maruts; see

Wonders unnumbered, Indian Prince!
    revealed to none save thee.

Behold! this is the Universe!—Look! what is
    live and dead

I gather all in one—in Me! Gaze, as thy lips
    have said,

On God Eternal, Very God! See Me! see
    what thou prayest!

   .   .   .   .

Thou canst not!—nor, with human eyes,
    Arjuna! ever mayest!

Therefore I give thee sense divine. Have
    other eyes, new light!

And, look! This is My glory, unveiled to
    mortal sight!

Sanjaya. Then, O King! the God, so
    saying,
Stood, to Pritha's Son displaying

All the splendor, wonder, dread
Of His vast Almighty-head.

Out of countless eyes beholding,
    Out of countless mouths commanding,
Countless mystic forms enfolding
    In one Form; supremely standing,

Countless radiant glories wearing,
Countless heavenly weapons bearing,

Crowned with garlands of star-clusters,
Robed in garb of woven lusters,

Breathing from His perfect Presence
Breaths of every subtle essence

Of all heavenly odors; shedding
Blinding brilliance; overspreading—

Boundless, beautiful—all spaces
With His all-regarding faces—

So He showed! If there should rise
Suddenly within the skies

Sunburst of a thousand suns
  Flooding earth with beams
    undeemed-of,
Then might be that Holy One's
  Majesty and radiance dreamed of!

  So did Pandu's Son behold
All this universe enfold

All its huge diversity
Into one vast shape, and be

Visible, and viewed, and blended
In one Body—subtle, splendid,

Nameless—th' All-comprehending
God of Gods, the Never-Ending
Deity!

      But, sore amazed,
Thrilled, o'erfilled, dazzled, and
    dazed,

Arjuna knelt, and bowed his head,
And clasped his palms and cried, and
    said:

  Arjuna. Yea! I have seen! I see!
    Lord! all is wrapped in Thee!

The gods are in Thy glorious frame! the
       creatures
    Of earth, and heaven, and hell
    In Thy Divine form dwell;
And in Thy countenance shine all the
       features

    Of Brahma, sitting lone
    Upon His lotus-throne;
Of saints and sages, and the serpent races
    Ananta, Vasuki;
    Yea! mightiest Lord! I see
Thy thousand thousand arms, and breasts,
      and faces,

    And eyes—on every side
    Perfect, diversified—
And nowhere end of Thee, nowhere
      beginning,
    Nowhere a center! Shifts—
    Wherever soul's gaze lifts—
Thy central Self, all-wielding, and all-
      winning!

    Infinite King! I see
    The anadem on Thee,

The club, the shell, the discus; see Thee
       burning
  In beams insufferable,
  Lighting earth, heaven, and hell
With brilliance blinding, glowing,
       flashing—turning

  Darkness to dazzling day,
  Look I whichever way.
Ah, Lord! I worship Thee—the Undivided,
  The Uttermost of thought,
  The Treasure-Palace wrought
To hold the wealth of the worlds, the Shield
      provided

  To shelter Virtue's laws,
  The Fount whence Life's stream draws
All waters of all rivers of all being;
  The One Unborn, Unending,
  Unchanging and Unblending!
With might and majesty, past thought, past
      seeing!

  Silver of moon and gold
  Of sun are glories rolled
From Thy great eyes—Thy visage, beaming
      tender

Throughout the stars and skies,
Doth to warm life surprise
Thy Universe. The worlds are filled with
wonder

Of Thy perfections! Space
Star-sprinkled, and void place
From pole to pole of the Blue, from bound to
bound,
Hath Thee in every spot—
Thee, Thee! Where Thou art not,
O Holy, Marvelous Form! is nowhere found!

O Mystic, Awful One!
At sight of Thee, made known,
The Three Worlds quake; the lower gods
draw nigh Thee,
They fold their palms, and bow
Body, and breast, and brow,
And, whispering worship, laud and magnify
Thee!

Rishis and Siddhas cry
"Hail! Highest Majesty!"
From sage and singer breaks the hymn of
glory

In dulcet harmony,
Sounding the praise of Thee;
While countless companies take up the
        story—

Rudras, who ride the storms,
Th' Adityas' shining forms,
Vasus and Sadhyas, Viswas, Ushmapas;
Maruts, and those great Twins,
The heavenly, fair Aswins,
Gandharvas, Rakshasas, Siddhas, and
        Asuras*—

These see Thee, and revere
In sudden-stricken fear;
Yea! the Worlds—seeing Thee with form
        stupendous,
With faces manifold,
With eyes which all behold,
Unnumbered eyes, vast arms, members
        tremendous,

Flanks, lit with sun and star,
Feet planted near and far,

* These are all divine or deified orders of the Hindu Pantheon.

Tushes of terror, mouths wrathful and
        tender—
    The Three wide Worlds before Thee
    Adore, as I adore Thee,
Quake, as I quake, to witness so much
        splendor!

    I mark Thee strike the skies
    With front in wondrous wise
Huge, rainbow-painted, glittering; and Thy
        mouth
    Opened, and orbs which see
    All things, whatever be
In all Thy worlds, east, west, and north and
        south.

    O Eyes of God! O Head!
    My strength of soul is fled;
Gone is heart's force, rebuked is mind's
        desire!
    When I behold Thee so,
    With awful brows a-glow,
With burning glance, and lips lighted by fire,

    Fierce as those flames which shall
    Consume, at close of all,

Earth, Heaven! Ah me! I see no Earth and
       Heaven!
    Thee, Lord of Lords! I see,
    Thee only—only Thee!
Now let Thy mercy unto me be given,

    Thou Refuge of the World!
    Lo! to the cavern hurled
Of Thy wide-opened throat, and lips white-
       tushed,
    I see our noblest ones,
    Great Dhritarashtra's sons,
Bhishma, Drona, and Karna, caught and
      crushed!

    The Kings and Chiefs drawn in,
    That gaping gorge within;
The best of both these armies torn and riven!
    Between Thy jaws they lie
    Mangled full bloodily,
Ground into dust and death! Like streams
      down-driven

    With helpless haste, which go
    In headlong furious flow

Straight to the gulfing deeps of th' unfilled
  ocean,
  So to that flaming cave
  Those heroes great and brave
Pour, in unending streams, with helpless
  motion!

  Like moths which in the night
  Flutter towards a light,
Drawn to their fiery doom, flying and dying,
  So to their death still throng,
  Blind, dazzled, borne along
Ceaselessly, all those multitudes, wild
  flying!

  Thou, that hast fashioned men,
  Devourest them again,
One with another, great and small, alike!
  The creatures whom Thou mak'st,
  With flaming jaws Thou tak'st,
Lapping them up! Lord God! Thy terrors
  strike

  From end to end of earth,
  Filling life full, from birth
To death, with deadly, burning, lurid dead!

Ah, Vishnu! make me know
Why is Thy visage so?
Who art Thou, feasting thus upon Thy dead!

Who? awful Deity!
I bow myself to Thee,
*Namostu Te, Devavara! Prasid!**
O Mightiest Lord! rehearse
Why hast Thou face so fierce?
Whence doth this aspect horrible proceed?

Krishna. Thou seest Me as Time who
    kills, Time who brings all to doom,
The Slayer Time, Ancient of Days, come
    hither to consume;

Excepting thee, of all these hosts of hostile
    chiefs arrayed,
There stands not one shall leave alive the
    battlefield! Dismayed

No longer be! Arise! obtain renown!
    destroy thy foes!
Fight for the kingdom waiting thee when
    thou hast vanquished those.

By Me they fall—not thee! the stroke of
    death is dealt them now,

* "Hail to Thee, God of Gods! Be favorable!"

Even as they show thus gallantly; My
    instrument art thou!

Strike, strong-armed Prince, at Drona! at
    Bhishma strike! deal death

On Karna, Jayadratha; stay all their warlike
    breath!

'Tis I who bid them perish! Thou wilt but
    slay the slain;

Fight! they must fall, and thou must live,
    victor upon this plain!

  Sanjaya. Hearing mighty Keshav's word,
    Tremblingly that helmèd Lord

    Clasped his lifted palms, and—praying
    Grace of Krishna—stood there, saying,

    With bowed brow and accents broken,
    These words, timorously spoken:

  Arjuna. Worthily, Lord of Might!
    The whole world hath delight

In Thy surpassing power, obeying Thee;
    The Rakshasas, in dread
    At sight of Thee, are sped

To all four quarters; and the company

    Of Siddhas sound Thy name.
    How should they not proclaim

Thy Majesties, Divinest, Mightiest?
    Thou Brahm, than Brahma greater!
    Thou Infinite Creator!
Thou God of gods, Life's Dwelling-place
    and Rest!

    Thou, of all souls the Soul!
    The Comprehending Whole!
Of Being formed, and formless Being the
    Framer;
    O Utmost One! O Lord!
    Older than eld, Who stored
The worlds with wealth of life! O Treasure-
    Claimer,

    Who wottest all, and art
    Wisdom Thyself! O Part
In all, and All; for all from Thee have risen!
    Numberless now I see
    The aspects are of Thee!
Vayu* Thou art, and He who keeps the prison

    Of Narak, Yama dark;
    And Agni's shining spark;
Varuna's waves are Thy waves. Moon and
    starlight

* The wind.

    Are Thine! Prajapati
    Art Thou, and 'tis to Thee
They knelt in worshiping the old world's
       far light,

    The first of mortal men.
    Again, Thou God! again
A thousand thousand times be magnified!
    Honor and worship be—
    Glory and praise—to Thee
Namo, Namaste, cried on every side;

    Cried here, above, below,
    Uttered when Thou dost go,
Uttered where Thou dost come! *Namo!* we
       call!
    Namostu! God adored!
    Namostu! Nameless Lord!
Hail to Thee! Praise to Thee! Thou One in all;

    For Thou art All! Yea, Thou!
    Ah! if in anger now
Thou shouldst remember I did think Thee
       Friend,
    Speaking with easy speech,
    As men use each to each;
Did call Thee "Krishna," "Prince," nor
       comprehend

Thy hidden majesty,
The might, the awe of Thee;
Did, in my heedlessness, or in my love,
On journey, or in jest,
Or when we lay at rest,
Sitting at council, straying in the grove,

Alone, or in the throng,
Do Thee, most Holy! wrong,
Be Thy grace granted for that witless sin!
For Thou art, now I know,
Father of all below,
Of all above, of all the worlds within,

Guru of Gurus, more
To reverence and adore
Than all which is adorable and high!
How, in the wide worlds three
Should any equal be?
Should any other share Thy Majesty?

Therefore, with body bent
And reverent intent,
I praise, and serve, and seek Thee, asking
grace.

As father to a son,
As friend to friend, as one
Who loveth to his lover, turn Thy face

In gentleness on me!
Good is it I did see
This unknown marvel of Thy Form! But fear
Mingles with joy! Retake,
Dear Lord! for pity's sake
Thine earthly shape, which earthly eyes
may bear!

Be merciful, and show
The visage that I know;
Let me regard Thee, as of yore, arrayed
With disc and forehead-gem,
With mace and anadem,
Thou that sustainest all things! Undismayed

Let me once more behold
The form I loved of old,
Thou of the thousand arms and countless
eyes!
This frightened heart is fain
To see restored again
My Charioteer, in Krishna's kind disguise.

Krishna. Yea! thou hast seen,
 Arjuna! because I loved thee well,
The secret countenance of Me, revealed by
 mystic spell,

Shining, and wonderful, and vast, majestic,
 manifold,
Which none save thou in all the years had
 favor to behold;

For not by Vedas cometh this, nor sacrifice,
 nor alms,
Nor works well-done, nor penance long, nor
 prayers, nor chanted psalms,

That mortal eyes should bear to view the
 Immortal Soul unclad,
Prince of the Kurus! This was kept for thee
 alone! Be glad!

Let no more trouble shake thy heart because
 thine eyes have seen
My terror with My glory. As I before have
 been

So will I be again for thee; with lightened
 heart behold!
Once more I am thy Krishna, the form thou
 knew'st of old!

Sanjaya. These words to Arjuna spake
  Vasudev, and straight did take

Back again the semblance dear
Of the well-loved charioteer;

Peace and joy it did restore
When the Prince beheld once more

Mighty BRAHMA'S form and face
Clothed in Krishna's gentle grace.

Arjuna. Now that I see come back,
  Janardana!
This friendly human frame, my mind can
  think
Calm thoughts once more; my heart beats
  still again!

Krishna. Yea! it was wonderful and
  terrible
To view me as thou didst, dear Prince! The
  Gods
Dread and desire continually to view!
Yet not by Vedas, nor from sacrifice,
Nor penance, nor gift-giving, nor with prayer
Shall any so behold, as thou hast seen!
Only by fullest service, perfect faith,

And uttermost surrender am I known
And seen, and entered into, Indian Prince!
Who doeth all for Me; who findeth Me
In all; adoreth always; loveth all
Which I have made, and Me, for Love's sole
    end,
That man, Arjuna! unto Me doth wend.

HERE ENDETH CHAPTER XI OF THE
BHAGAVAD-GITA,

Entitled "Viswarupadarsanam,"
Or "The Book of the Manifesting of the One
and Manifold."

CHAPTER XII

The Religion of Faith

Arjuna. Lord! of the men who serve
    Thee—true in heart—
As God revealed; and of the men who serve,
Worshiping Thee Unrevealed, Unbodied,
    Far,
Which take the better way of faith and life?

Krishna. Whoever serve Me—as I show
    Myself—
Constantly true, in full devotion fixed,
Those hold I very holy. But who serve,
Worshiping Me, The One, The Invisible,
The Unrevealed, Unnamed, Unthinkable,
Uttermost, All-pervading, Highest, Sure—
Who thus adore Me, mastering their senses,
Of one set mind to all, glad in all good,
These blessèd souls come unto Me.

                    Yet, hard
The travail is for such as bend their minds
To reach th' Unmanifest. That viewless path
Shall scarce be trod by man bearing the
    flesh!

But whereso any doeth all his deeds
Renouncing self for Me, full of Me, fixed
To serve only the Highest, night and day
Musing on Me—him will I swiftly lift
Forth from life's ocean of distress and death
Whose soul clings fast to Me. Cling thou to
    Me!
Clasp Me with heart and mind! so shalt thou
    dwell
Surely with Me on high. But if thy thought
Droops from such height; if thou be'st weak
    to set
Body and soul upon Me constantly,
Despair not! give Me lower service! seek
To reach Me, worshiping with steadfast will;
And, if thou canst not worship steadfastly,
Work for Me, toil in works pleasing to Me!
For he that laboreth right for love of Me
Shall finally attain! But, if in this
Thy faint heart fails, bring Me thy failure!
    find
Refuge in Me! let fruits of labor go,
Renouncing hope for Me, with lowliest
    heart,
So shalt thou come; for, though to know is
    more

Than diligence, yet worship better is
Than knowing, and renouncing better still.
Near to renunciation—very near—
Dwelleth Eternal Peace!

                        Who hateth naught
Of all which lives, living himself benign,
Compassionate, from arrogance exempt,
Exempt from love of self, unchangeable
By good or ill; patient, contented, firm
In faith, mastering himself, true to his word,
Seeking Me, heart and soul; vowed unto
      Me—
That man I love! Who troubleth not his kind,
And is not troubled by them; clear of wrath,
Living too high for gladness, grief, or fear,
That man I love! Who, dwelling quiet-eyed,*
Stainless, serene, well-balanced,
      unperplexed,
Working with Me, yet from all works
      detached,
That man I love! Who, fixed in faith on Me,
Dotes upon none, scorns none; rejoices not,
And grieves not, letting good or evil hap
Light when it will, and when it will depart,

* "Not peering about," *anapeksha.*

That man I love! Who, unto friend and foe
Keeping an equal heart, with equal mind
Bears shame and glory; with an equal peace
Takes heat and cold, pleasure and pain;
    abides
Quit of desires, hears praise or calumny
In passionless restraint, unmoved by each,
Linked by no ties to earth, steadfast in Me,
That man I love! But most of all I love
Those happy ones to whom 'tis life to live
In single fervid faith and love unseeing,
Drinking the blessèd Amrit of my Being!

HERE ENDETH CHAPTER XII OF THE
BHAGAVAD-GITA,

Entitled "Bhaktiyog,"
Or "The Book of the Religion of Faith."

CHAPTER XIII

Religion by Separation of Matter and Spirit

Arjuna. Now would I hear, O gracious
    Kesava!*
Of Life which seems, and Soul beyond, which
    sees,
And what it is we know—or think to know.

Krishna. Yea! Son of Kunti! for this flesh
    ye see
Is *Kshetra,* is the field where Life disports;
And that which views and knows it is the
    Soul,
Kshetrajna. In all "fields," thou Indian
    prince!
I am *Kshetrajna.* I am what surveys!
Only that knowledge knows which knows
    the known
By the knower! What it is, that "field" of
    life,
What qualities it hath, and whence it is,

* The Calcutta edition of the Mahabharata has
these three opening lines.

And why it changeth, and the faculty
That wotteth it, the mightiness of this,
And how it wotteth—hear these things from
    Me!

   .   .   .   .   .   *

  The elements, the conscious life, the
    mind,
The unseen vital force, the nine strange
    gates
Of the body, and the five domains of sense;
Desire, dislike, pleasure and pain, and
    thought
Deep-woven, and persistency of being;
These all are wrought on Matter by the Soul!

  Humbleness, truthfulness, and
    harmlessness,
Patience and honor, reverence for the wise,
Purity, constancy, control of self,
Contempt of sense-delights, self-sacrifice,
Perception of the certitude of ill
In birth, death, age, disease, suffering, and
    sin;

* I omit two lines of the Sanskrit here, evidently
interpolated by some Vedantist.

Detachment, lightly holding unto home,
Children, and wife, and all that bindeth
    men;
An ever-tranquil heart in fortunes good
And fortunes evil, with a will set firm
To worship Me—Me only! ceasing not;
Loving all solitudes, and shunning noise
Of foolish crowds; endeavors resolute
To reach perception of the Utmost Soul,
And grace to understand what gain it were
So to attain—this is true Wisdom, Prince!
And what is otherwise is ignorance!

  Now will I speak of knowledge best to
    know—
That Truth which giveth man Amrit to drink,
The Truth of HIM, the Para-Brahm, the All,
The Uncreated; not *Asat*, not *Sat*,
Not Form, nor the Unformed; yet both, and
    more—
Whose hands are everywhere, and
    everywhere
Planted His feet, and everywhere His eyes
Beholding, and His ears in every place
Hearing, and all His faces everywhere
Enlightening and encompassing His worlds.

Glorified in the senses He hath given,
Yet beyond sense He is; sustaining all,
Yet dwells He unattached: of forms and
    modes
Master, yet neither form nor mode hath He;
He is within all beings—and without—
Motionless, yet still moving; not discerned
For subtlety of instant presence; close
To all, to each, yet measurelessly far!
Not manifold, and yet subsisting still
In all which lives; forever to be known
As the Sustainer, yet, at the End of Times,
He maketh all to end—and re-creates.
The Light of Lights He is, in the heart of the
    Dark
Shining eternally. Wisdom He is
And Wisdom's way, and Guide of all the
    wise,
Planted in every heart.

                So have I told
Of Life's stuff, and the moulding, and the
    lore
To comprehend. Whoso, adoring Me,
Perceiveth this, shall surely come to Me!

   Know thou that Nature and the Spirit
    both

Have no beginning! Know that qualities
And changes of them are by Nature wrought;
That Nature puts to work the acting frame,
But Spirit doth inform it, and so cause
Feeling of pain and pleasure. Spirit, linked
To moulded matter, entereth into bond
With qualities by Nature framed, and, thus
Married to matter, breeds the birth again
In good or evil *yonis.**

             Yet is this—
Yea! in its bodily prison!—Spirit pure,
Spirit supreme; surveying, governing,
Guarding, possessing; Lord and Master still
PURUSHA, Ultimate, One Soul with Me.

  Whoso thus knows himself, and knows
    his soul
PURUSHA, working through the qualities
With Nature's modes, the light hath come
    for him!
Whatever flesh he bears, never again
Shall he take on its load. Some few there be
By meditation find the Soul in Self
Self-schooled; and some by long philosophy
And holy life reach thither; some by works.

* Wombs.

Some, never so attaining, hear of light
From other lips, and seize, and cleave to it
Worshiping; yea! and those—to teaching
    true—
Overpass Death!

               Wherever, Indian Prince!
Life is—of moving things, or things
    unmoved,
Plant or still seed—know, what is there hath
    grown
By bond of Matter and of Spirit: Know
He sees indeed who sees in all alike
The living, lordly Soul; the Soul Supreme,
Imperishable amid the Perishing:
For, whoso thus beholds, in every place,
In every form, the same, one, Living Lord,
Doth no more wrongfulness unto himself,
But goes the highest road which brings to
    bliss.
Seeing, he sees, indeed, who sees that works
Are Nature's wont, for Soul to practice by
Acting, yet not the agent; sees the mass
Of separate living things—each of its kind—
Issue from One, and blend again to One:
Then hath he BRAHMA, he attains!

O Prince!
That Ultimate, High Spirit, Uncreate,
Unqualified, even when it entereth flesh
Taketh no stain of acts, worketh in naught!
Like to th' ethereal air, pervading all,
Which, for sheer subtlety, avoideth taint,
The subtle Soul sits everywhere, unstained:
Like to the light of the all-piercing sun
[Which is not changed by aught it shines
    upon]
The Soul's light shineth pure in every place;
And they who, by such eye of wisdom, see
How Matter, and what deals with it, divide;
And how the Spirit and the flesh have strife,
Those wise ones go the way which leads to
    Life!

HERE ENDETH CHAPTER XIII OF THE
BHAGAVAD-GITA,

Entitled "Kshetrakshetrajnavibhagayog,"
Or "The Book of Religion by Separation of
Matter and Spirit."

CHAPTER XIV

Religion by Separation from the Qualities

Krishna. Yet farther will I open unto thee
This wisdom of all wisdoms, uttermost,
The which possessing, all My saints have
    passed
To perfectness. On such high verities
Reliant, rising into fellowship
With Me, they are not born again at birth
Of *Kalpas*, nor at *Pralayas* suffer change!

This Universe the Womb is where I plant
Seed of all lives! Thence, Prince of India,
    comes
Birth to all beings! Whoso, Kunti's Son!
Mothers each mortal form, Brahma con-
    ceives,
And I am He that fathers, sending seed!

Sattwa, Rajas, and *Tamas*—so are named
The qualities of Nature—"Soothfastness,"
"Passion," and "Ignorance." These three
    bind down

The changeless Spirit in the changeful
    flesh.
Whereof sweet "Soothfastness," by purity
Living unsullied and enlightened, binds
The sinless Soul to happiness and truth;
And Passion, being kin to appetite
And breeding impulse and propensity,
Binds the embodied Soul, O Kunti's Son!
By tie of works. But Ignorance, begot
Of Darkness, blinding mortal men, binds
    down
Their souls to stupor, sloth, and drowsiness.
Yea, Prince of India! Soothfastness binds
    souls
In pleasant wise to flesh; and Passion binds
By toilsome strain; but Ignorance, which
    blots
The beams of wisdom, binds the soul to
    sloth.
Passion and Ignorance, once overcome,
Leave Soothfastness, O Bharata! Where this
With Ignorance are absent, Passion rules;
And Ignorance in hearts not good nor quick.
When at all gateways of the Body shines
The Lamp of Knowledge, then may one see
    well

Soothfastness settled in that city reigns;
Where longing is, and ardor, and unrest,
Impulse to strive and gain, and avarice,
Those spring from Passion—Prince!—
    engrained; and where
Darkness and dullness, sloth and stupor
    are,
'Tis Ignorance hath caused them, Kuru
    Chief!

  Moreover, when a soul departeth, fixed
In Soothfastness, it goeth to the place—
Perfect and pure—of those that know all
    Truth.
If it departeth in set habitude
Of Impulse, it shall pass into the world
Of spirits tied to works; and, if it dies
In hardened Ignorance, that blinded soul
Is born anew in some unlighted womb.

  The fruit of Soothfastness is true and
    sweet;
The fruit of lusts is pain and toil; the fruit
Of Ignorance is deeper darkness. Yea!
For Light brings light, and Passion ache to
    have.
And gloom, bewilderments, and ignorance

Grow forth from Ignorance. Those of the first
Rise ever higher; those of the second mode
Take a mid place; the darkened souls sink
　　back
To lower deeps, loaded with witlessness!

　When, watching life, the living man
　　perceives
The only actors are the Qualities,
And knows what rules beyond the Qualities,
Then is he come nigh unto Me!

　　　　　　　　　　　　　The Soul,
Thus passing forth from the Three
　　Qualities—
Whereby arise all bodies—overcomes
Birth, Death, Sorrow, and Age; and drinketh
　　deep
The undying wine of Amrit.

　Arjuna.　　　　　　　Oh! my Lord!
Which be the signs to know him that hath
　　gone
Past the Three Modes? How liveth he?
　　What way
Leadeth him safe beyond the threefold
　　Modes?

Krishna. He who with equanimity
    surveys
Luster of goodness, strife of passion, sloth
Of ignorance, not angry if they are,
Not wishful when they are not: he who sits
A sojourner and stranger in their midst
Unruffled, standing off, saying—serene—
When troubles break, "These be the
    Qualities!"
He unto whom—Self-centered—grief and
    joy
Sound as one word; to whose deep-seeing
    eyes
The clod, the marble, and the gold are one;
Whose equal heart holds the same gentleness
For lovely and unlovely things, firm-set,
Well-pleased in praise and dispraise;
    satisfied
With honor or dishonor; unto friends
And unto foes alike in tolerance,
Detached from undertakings—he is named
Surmounter of the Qualities!

                              And such—
With single, fervent faith adoring Me,
Passing beyond the Qualities, conforms

To Brahma, and attains Me!

For I am
That whereof Brahma is the likeness! Mine
The Amrit is; and Immortality
Is mine; and mine perfect Felicity!

HERE ENDETH CHAPTER XIV OF THE
BHAGAVAD-GITA,

Entitled "Gunatrayavibhagayog,"
Or "The Book of Religion by Separation
from the Qualities."

CHAPTER XV

Religion by Attaining the Supreme

Krishna. Men call the Aswattha—the
    Banyan-tree—
Which hath its boughs beneath, its roots
    above—
The ever-holy tree. Yea! for its leaves
Are green and waving hymns which whisper
    Truth!
Who knows the Aswattha, knows Veds, and
    all.

Its branches shoot to heaven and sink to
    earth.*
Even as the deeds of men, which take their
    birth
    From qualities: its silver sprays and
    blooms,

* I do not consider the Sanskrit verses here—
which are somewhat freely rendered—"an attack
on the authority of the Vedas," with Mr. Davies,
but a beautiful lyrical episode, a new "Par-
able of the fig tree."

And all the eager verdure of its girth,

Leap to quick life at kiss of sun and air,
As men's lives quicken to the temptings fair
   Of wooing sense: its hanging rootlets
     seek
The soil beneath, helping to hold it there,

As actions wrought amid this world of men
Bind them by ever-tightening bonds again.
   If ye knew well the teaching of the Tree,
What its shape saith; and whence it springs;
     and, then

How it must end, and all the ills of it,
The axe of sharp Detachment ye would whet,
   And cleave the clinging snaky roots,
     and lay
This Aswattha of sense-life low—to set

New growths upspringing to that happier
     sky—
Which they who reach shall have no day to
     die,
   Nor fade away, nor fall—to Him, I mean,
FATHER and FIRST, Who made the mystery

Of old Creation; for to Him come they
From passion and from dreams who break
    away;
  Who part the bonds constraining them
    to flesh,
And—Him, the Highest, worshiping alway—

No longer grow at mercy of what breeze
Of summer pleasure stirs the sleeping trees,
  What blast of tempest tears them, bough
    and stem.
To the eternal world pass such as these!

Another Sun gleams there! another Moon!
Another Light—not Dusk, nor Dawn, nor
    Noon—
  Which they who once behold return no
    more;
They have attained My rest, life's Utmost
    boon!

  When, in this world of manifested life,
The undying Spirit, setting forth from Me,
Taketh on form, it draweth to itself
From Being's storehouse—which containeth
    all—

Senses and intellect. The Sovereign Soul
Thus entering the flesh, or quitting it,
Gathers these up, as the wind gathers scents,
Blowing above the flower-beds. Ear and Eye,
And Touch and Taste, and Smelling, these
    it takes—
Yea, and a sentient mind—linking itself
To sense-things so.

                 The unenlightened ones
Mark not that Spirit when he goes or comes,
Nor when he takes his pleasure in the form,
Conjoined with qualities; but those see plain
Who have the eyes to see. Holy souls see
Which strive thereto, Enlightened,
    they perceive
That Spirit in themselves; but foolish ones,
Even though they strive, discern not, having
    hearts
Unkindled, ill—informed!

                 Know, too, from Me
Shineth the gathered glory of the suns
Which lighten all the world: from Me the
    moons
Draw silvery beams, and fire fierce
    loveliness.

I penetrate the clay, and lend all shapes
Their living force; I glide into the plant—
Root, leaf, and bloom—to make the wood-
    lands green
With springing sap. Becoming vital warmth,
I glow in glad, respiring frames, and pass
With outward and with inward breath to
    feed
The body by all meats.*

                For in this world
Being is twofold: the Divided, one;
The Undivided, one. All things that live
Are "the Divided." That which sits apart,
"The Undivided."

            Higher still is He,
The Highest, holding all, whose Name is
    LORD,
The Eternal, Sovereign, First! Who fills all
    worlds,
Sustaining them. And—dwelling thus
    beyond
Divided Being and Undivided—I
Am called of men and Vedas, Life Supreme,
The PURUSHOTTAMA.

* I omit a verse here, evidently interpolated.

Who knows Me thus,
With mind unclouded, knoweth all, dear
    Prince!
And with his whole soul ever worshipeth
    Me.

Now is the sacred, secret Mystery
Declared to thee! Who comprehendeth this
Hath wisdom! He is quit of works in bliss!

HERE ENDETH CHAPTER XV OF THE
BHAGAVAD-GITA,

Entitled "Purushottamapraptiyog,"
Or "The Book of Religion by attaining
the Supreme."

CHAPTER XVI

The Separateness of the Divine and Undivine

Krishna. Fearlessness, singleness of soul,
    the will
Always to strive for wisdom; opened hand
And governed appetites; and piety
And love of lonely study; humbleness,
Uprightness, heed to injure naught which
    lives,
Truthfulness, slowness unto wrath, a mind
That lightly letteth go what others prize;
And equanimity, and charity
Which spieth no man's faults; and tenderness
Towards all that suffer; a contented heart,
Fluttered by no desires; a bearing mild,
Modest, and grave, with manhood
    nobly mixed,
With patience, fortitude, and purity;
An unrevengeful spirit, never given
To rate itself too high—such be the signs,
O Indian Prince! of him whose feet are set
On that fair path which leads to heavenly
    birth!

Deceitfulness, and arrogance, and pride,
Quickness to anger, harsh and evil speech,
And ignorance, to its own darkness blind—
These be the signs, My Prince! of him whose
    birth
Is fated for the regions of the vile.*

The Heavenly Birth brings to deliverance,
So should'st thou know! The birth with
    Asuras
Brings into bondage. Be thou joyous, Prince!
Whose lot is set apart for heavenly Birth.

Two stamps there are marked on all living
    men,
Divine and Undivine; I spake to thee
By what marks thou shouldst know the
    Heavenly Man,
Hear from me now of the Unheavenly!

They comprehend not, the Unheavenly,
How Souls go forth from Me; nor how they
    come
Back unto Me: nor is there Truth in these,
Nor purity, or rule of Life. "This world

* "Of the Asuras," lit.

Hath not a Law, nor Order, nor a Lord,"
So say they: "Nor hath risen up by Cause
Following on Cause, in perfect purposing,
But is none other than a House of Lust."
And, this thing thinking, all those ruined
    ones—
Of little wit, dark-minded—give themselves
To evil deeds, the curses of their kind.
Surrendered to desires insatiable,
Full of deceitfulness, folly, and pride,
In blindness cleaving to their errors, caught
Into the sinful course, they trust this lie
As it were true—this lie which leads to
    death—
Finding in Pleasure all the good which is,
And crying "Here it finisheth!"

                  Ensnared
In nooses of a hundred idle hopes,
Slaves to their passion and their wrath, they
    buy
Wealth with base deeds, to glut hot
    appetites;
"Thus much, today," they say, "we gained!
    thereby
Such and such wish of heart shall have its
    fill;

And this is ours! and th' other shall be ours!
Today we slew a foe, and we will slay
Our other enemy tomorrow! Look!
Are we not lords? Make we not goodly cheer?
Is not our fortune famous, brave, and great?
Rich are we, proudly born! What other men
Live like to us? Kill, then, for sacrifice!
Cast largesse, and be merry!'' So they speak
Darkened by ignorance; and so they fall—
Tossed to and fro with projects, tricked, and
    bound
In net of black delusion, lost in lusts—
Down to foul Naraka. Conceited, fond,
Stubborn and proud, dead-drunken with
    wine
Of wealth, and reckless, all their offerings
Have but a show of reverence, being not
    made
In piety of ancient faith. Thus vowed
To self-hood, force, insolence, feasting,
    wrath,
These My blasphemers, in the forms they
    wear
And in the forms they breed, my foemen are,
Hateful and hating; cruel, evil, vile,
Lowest and least of men, whom I cast down

Again, and yet again, at end of lives,
Into some devilish womb, whence—birth
    by birth—
The devilish wombs re-spawn them, all
    beguiled;
And, till they find and worship Me, sweet
    Prince!
Tread they that Nether Road.

                The Doors of Hell
Are threefold, whereby men to ruin pass—
The door of Lust, the door of Wrath, the door
Of Avarice. Let a man shun those three!
He who shall turn aside from entering
All those three gates of Narak, wendeth
    straight
To find his peace, and comes to Swarga's
    gate.

   .   .   .   .   .   *

HERE ENDETH CHAPTER XVI OF THE
BHAGAVAD-GITA,

Entitled "Daivasarasaupadwibhagayog,"
Or "The Book of the Separateness of the
Divine and Undivine."

* I omit the ten concluding slokas, with Mr.
Davies.

CHAPTER XVII

Religion by the Threefold Kinds of Faith

Arjuna. If men forsake the holy
    ordinance,
Heedless of Shastras, yet keep faith at heart
And worship, what shall be the state of those,
Great Krishna! *Sattwan, Rajas, Tamas?* Say!

Krishna. Threefold the faith is of man-
    kind, and springs
From those three qualities—becoming
    "true,"
Or "passion-stained," or "dark," as thou shalt
    hear!

The faith of each believer, Indian Prince!
Conforms itself to what he truly is.
Where thou shalt see a worshiper, that one
To what he worships lives assimilate:
[Such as the shrine, so is the votary],
The "soothfast" souls adore true gods; the
    souls

Obeying *Rajas* worship Rakshasas*
Or Yakshas; and the men of Darkness pray
To Pretas and to Bhutas.† Yea, and those
Who practice bitter penance, not enjoined
By rightful rule—penance which hath its
    root
In self-sufficient, proud hypocrisies—
Those men, passion-beset, violent, wild,
Torturing—the witless ones—My elements
Shut in fair company within their flesh,
(Nay, Me myself, present within the flesh!)
Know them to devils devoted, not to
    Heaven!
For like as foods are threefold for mankind
In nourishing, so is there threefold way
Of worship, abstinence, and almsgiving!
Hear this of Me! there is a food which brings
Force, substance, strength, and health, and
    joy to live,
Being well-seasoned, cordial, comforting,
The "Soothfast" meat. And there be foods
    which bring

* Rakshasas and Yakshas are unembodied but
capricious beings of great power, gifts, and beauty,
sometimes also of benignity.

† These are spirits of evil, wandering ghosts.

Aches and unrests, and burning blood, and
    grief,
Being too biting, heating, salt, and sharp,
And therefore craved by too strong appetite.
And there is foul food—kept from over-
    night,*
Savorless, filthy, which the foul will eat,
A feast of rottenness, meet for the lips
Of such as love the "Darkness."

               Thus with rites—
A sacrifice not for rewardment made,
Offered in rightful wise, when he who vows
Sayeth, with heart devout, "This I should
    do!"
Is "Soothfast" rite. But sacrifice for gain,
Offered for good repute, be sure that this,
O Best of Bharatas! is Rajas-rite,
With stamp of "passion." And a sacrifice
Offered against the laws, with no due dole
Of food-giving, with no accompaniment
Of hallowed hymn, nor largesse to the
    priests,

* *Yatayaman,* food which has remained after the
watches of the night. In India this would probably
"go bad."

In faithless celebration, call it vile,
The deed of "Darkness!"—lost!

                        Worship of gods
Meriting worship; lowly reverence
Of Twice-borns, Teachers, Elders; Purity,
Rectitude, and the Brahmacharya's vow,
And not to injure any helpless thing—
These make a true religiousness of Act.

  Words causing no man woe, words ever
     true,
Gentle and pleasing words, and those ye say
In murmured reading of Sacred Writ—
These maketh true religiousness of Speech.

  Serenity of soul, benignity,
Sway of the silent Spirit, constant stress
To sanctify the Nature—these things make
Good rite, and true religiousness of Mind.

  Such threefold faith, in highest piety
Kept, with no hope of gain, by hearts devote
Is perfect work of *Sattwan*, true belief.

  Religion shown in act of proud display
To win good entertainment, worship, fame,

Such—say I—is of *Rajas*, rash and vain.

Religion followed by a witless will
To torture self, or come at power to hurt
Another—'tis of *Tamas*, dark and ill.

The gift lovingly given, when one shall
     say
"Now must I gladly give!" when he who
     takes
Can render nothing back; made in due place,
Due time, and to a meet recipient,
Is gift of *Sattwan*, fair and profitable.

The gift selfishly given, where to receive
Is hoped again, or when some end is sought,
Or where the gift is proffered with a grudge,
This is of *Rajas*, stained with impulse, ill.

The gift churlishly flung, at evil time,
In wrongful place, to base recipient,
Made in disdain or harsh unkindliness,
Is gift of *Tamas*, dark; it doth not bless!*

* I omit the concluding *slokas*, as of very doubtful authenticity.

HERE ENDETH CHAPTER XVII OF THE
BHAGAVAD-GITA,

Entitled "Sraddhatrayavibhagayog,"
Or "The Book of Religion by the Threefold
Kinds of Faith."

CHAPTER XVIII

Religion by Deliverance and Renunciation

Arjuna. Fain would I better know, Thou
    Glorious One!
The very truth—Heart's Lord!—of *Sannyas*,
Abstention; and Renunciation, Lord!
Tyaga; and what separates these twain!
    Krishna. The poets rightly teach that
        Sannyas
Is the forgoing of all acts which spring
Out of desire; and their wisest say
Tyaga is renouncing fruit of acts.

There be among the saints some who have
    held
All action sinful, and to be renounced;
And some who answer, "Nay! the goodly
    acts—
As worship, penance, alms—must be
    performed!"
Hear now My sentence, Best of Bharatas!

'Tis well set forth, O Chaser of thy Foes!
Renunciation is of threefold form,
And Worship, Penance, Alms, not to be
        stayed;
Nay, to be gladly done; for all those three
Are purifying waters for true souls!

Yet must be practiced even those high
        works
In yielding up attachment, and all fruit
Produced by works. This is My judgment,
        Prince!
This My insuperable and fixed decree!

Abstaining from a work by right
        prescribed
Never is meet! So to abstain doth spring
From "darkness," and Delusion teacheth it.
Abstaining from a work grievous to flesh,
When one saith "'Tis unpleasing!" this is
        null!
Such an one acts from "passion"; naught of
        gain
Wins his Renunciation! But, Arjun!
Abstaining from attachment to the work,
Abstaining from rewardment in the work,

While yet one doeth it full faithfully,
Saying, " 'Tis right to do!" that is "true" act
And abstinence! Who doeth duties so,
Unvexed if his work fail, if it succeed
Unflattered, in his own heart justified,
Quit of debates and doubts, his is "true" act:
For, being in the body, none may stand
Wholly aloof from act; yet, who abstains
From profit of his acts is abstinent.

    The fruit of labors, in the lives to come,
Is threefold for all men—Desirable,
And Undesirable, and mixed of both;
But no fruit is at all where no work was.

    Hear from me, Long-armed Lord! the
      makings five
Which go to every act, in Sankhya taught
As necessary. First the force; and then
The agent; next, the various instruments;
Fourth, the especial effort; fifth, the God.
What work soever any mortal doth
Of body, mind, or speech, evil or good,
By these five doth he that. Which being thus,
Whoso, for lack of knowledge, seeth himself
As the sole actor, knoweth naught at all
And seeth naught. Therefore, I say, if one—

Holding aloof from self—with unstained
    mind
Should slay all yonder host, being bid to
    slay,
He doth not slay; he is not bound thereby!

  Knowledge, the thing known, and the
    mind which knows,
These make the threefold starting-ground of
    act.
The act, the actor, and the instrument,
These make the threefold total of the deed.
But knowledge, agent, act, are differenced
By three dividing qualities. Hear now
Which be the qualities dividing them.

  There is "true" Knowledge. Learn thou
    it is this:
To see one changeless Life in all the Lives,
And in the Separate, One Inseparable.
There is imperfect Knowledge: that which
    sees
The separate existences apart,
And, being separated, holds them real.
There is false Knowledge: that which blindly
    clings

To one as if 'twere all, seeking no Cause,
Deprived of light, narrow, and dull, and
    "dark."

  There is "right" Action: that which—
      being enjoined—
Is wrought without attachment,
      passionlessly,
For duty, not for love, nor hate, nor gain.
There is "vain" Action: that which men
      pursue
Aching to satisfy desires, impelled
By sense of self, with all-absorbing stress:
This is of *Rajas*—passionate and vain.
There is "dark" Action: when one doth a
      thing
Heedless of issues, heedless of the hurt
Or wrong for others, heedless if he harm
His own soul—'tis of *Tamas*, black and bad!

  There is the "rightful" doer. He who acts
Free from self-seeking, humble, resolute,
Steadfast, in good or evil hap the same,
Content to do aright—he "truly" acts.
There is th' "impassioned" doer. He that
      works

From impulse, seeking profit, rude and bold
To overcome, unchastened; slave by turns
Of sorrow and of joy: of *Rajas* he!
And there be evil doers; loose of heart,
Low-minded, stubborn, fraudulent, remiss,
Dull, slow, despondent—children of the
    "dark."

Hear, too, of Intellect and Steadfastness
The threefold separation, Conqueror-Prince!
How these are set apart by Qualities.

Good is the Intellect which comprehends
The coming forth and going back of life,
What must be done, and what must not be
    done,
What should be feared, and what should not
    be feared,
What binds and what emancipates the soul:
That is of *Sattwan*, Prince! of
    "soothfastness."
Marred is the Intellect which, knowing right
And knowing wrong, and what is well to do
And what must not be done, yet understands
Naught with firm mind, nor as the calm
    truth is:

This is of *Rajas*, Prince! and "passionate!"
Evil is Intellect which, wrapped in gloom,
Looks upon wrong as right, and sees all
    things
Contrariwise of Truth. O Pritha's Son!
That is of *Tamas*, "dark" and desperate!

   Good is the steadfastness whereby a man
Masters his beats of heart, his very breath
Of life, the action of his senses; fixed
In never-shaken faith and piety:
That is of *Sattwan*, Prince! "soothfast" and
    fair!
Stained is the steadfastness whereby a man
Holds to his duty, purpose, effort, end,
For life's sake, and the love of goods to gain,
Arjuna! 'tis of *Rajas*, passion-stamped!
Sad is the steadfastness wherewith the fool
Cleaves to his sloth, his sorrow, and his fears,
His folly and despair. This—Pritha's Son!—
Is born of *Tamas*, "dark" and miserable!

   Hear further, Chief of Bharatas! from Me
The threefold kinds of Pleasure which there
    be.

Good Pleasure is the pleasure that
    endures,
Banishing pain for aye; bitter at first
As poison to the soul, but afterward
Sweet as the taste of Amrit. Drink of that!
It springeth in the Spirit's deep content.
And painful Pleasure springeth from the
    bond
Between the senses and the sense-world.
    Sweet
As Amrit is its first taste, but its last
Bitter as poison. 'Tis of *Rajas*, Prince!
And foul and "dark" the pleasure is which
    springs
From sloth and sin and foolishness; at first
And at the last, and all the way of life
The soul bewildering. 'Tis of *Tamas*, Prince!

For nothing lives on earth, nor 'midst the
    gods
In utmost heaven, but hath its being bound
With these three Qualities, by Nature
    framed.

The work of Brahmans, Kshatriyas, Vaisyas,
And Sudras, O thou Slayer of thy Foes!

Is fixed by reason of the Qualities
Planted in each:

            A Brahman's virtues, Prince!
Born of his nature, are serenity,
Self-mastery, religion, purity,
Patience, uprightness, learning, and to know
The truth of things which be. A Kshatriya's
     pride,
Born of his nature, lives in valor, fire,
Constancy, skillfulness, spirit in fight,
And open-handedness and noble mien,
As a lord of men. A Vaisya's task,
Born with his nature, is to till the ground,
Tend cattle, venture trade. A Sudra's state,
Suiting his nature, is to minister.

   Whoso performeth—diligent, content—
The work allotted him, whate'er it be,
Lays hold of perfectness! Hear how a man
Findeth perfection, being so content:
He findeth it through worship—wrought by
     work—
Of HIM that is the Source of all which lives.
Of HIM by Whom the universe was stretched.

Better thine own work is, though done
    with fault,
Than doing others' work, ev'n excellently.
He shall not fall in sin who fronts the task
Set him by Nature's hand! Let no man leave
His natural duty, Prince! though it bear
    blame!
For every work hath blame, as every flame
Is wrapped in smoke! Only that man attains
Perfect surcease of work whose work was
    wrought
With mind unfettered, soul wholly subdued,
Desires forever dead, results renounced.

  Learn from me, Son of Kunti! also this,
How one, attaining perfect peace, attains
BRAHM, the supreme, the highest height
    of all!

  Devoted—with a heart grown pure,
    restrained
In lordly self-control, forgoing wiles
Of song and senses, freed from love and hate,
Dwelling 'mid solitudes, in diet spare,
With body, speech, and will tamed to obey,

Ever to holy meditation vowed,
From passions liberate, quit of the Self,
Of arrogance, impatience, anger, pride;
Freed from surroundings, quiet, lacking
    naught—
Such an one grows to oneness with the
    BRAHM;
Such an one, growing one with BRAHM,
    serene,
Sorrows no more, desires no more; his soul,
Equally loving all that lives, loves well
Me, Who have made them, and attains to Me.
By this same love and worship doth he know
Me as I am, how high and wonderful,
And knowing, straightway enters into Me.
And whatsoever deeds he doeth—fixed
In Me, as in his refuge—he hath won
Forever and forever by My grace
Th' Eternal Rest! So win thou! In thy
    thoughts,
Do all thou dost for Me! Renounce for Me!
Sacrifice heart and mind and will to Me!
Live in the faith of Me! In faith of Me
All dangers thou shalt vanquish, by My
    grace;
But, trusting to thyself and heeding not,

Thou can'st but perish! If this day thou
    say'st,
Relying on thyself, "I will not fight!"
Vain will the purpose prove! thy qualities
Would spur thee to the war. What thou dost
    shun,
Misled by fair illusions, thou wouldst seek
Against thy will, when the task comes to thee
Waking the promptings in thy nature set.
There lives a Master in the hearts of men
Maketh their deeds, by subtle pulling-
    strings,
Dance to what tune HE will. With all thy soul
Trust Him, and take Him for thy succor,
    Prince!
So—only so, Arjuna!—shalt thou gain—
By grace of Him—the uttermost repose,
The Eternal Place!
                    Thus hath been opened thee
This Truth of Truths, the Mystery more hid
Than any secret mystery. Meditate!
And—as thou wilt—then act!

                    Nay! but once more
Take My last word, My utmost meaning
    have!

Precious thou art to Me; right well-beloved!
Listen! I tell thee for thy comfort this.
Give Me thy heart! adore Me! serve Me! cling
In faith and love and reverence to Me!
So shalt thou come to Me! I promise true,
For thou art sweet to Me

                  And let go those—
Rites and writ duties! Fly to Me alone!
Make Me thy single refuge! I will free
Thy soul from all its sins! Be of good cheer!

> [Hide, the holy Krishna saith,
> This from him that hath no faith,
>
> Him that worships not, nor seeks
> Wisdom's teaching when she speaks:
>
> Hide it from all men who mock;
> But, wherever, 'mid the flock
>
> Of My lovers, one shall teach
> This divinest, wisest, speech—
>
> Teaching in the faith to bring
> Truth to them, and offering
>
> Of all honor unto Me—
> Unto Brahma cometh he!
>
> Nay, and nowhere shall ye find

Any man of all mankind

Doing dearer deed for Me;
Nor shall any dearer be

In My earth. Yea, furthermore,
Whoso reads this converse o'er,

Held by Us upon the plain,
Pondering piously and fain,

He hath paid Me sacrifice!
(Krishna speaketh in this wise!)

Yea, and whoso, full of faith,
Heareth wisely what it saith,

Heareth meekly—when he dies,
Surely shall his spirit rise

To those regions where the Blest,
Free of flesh, in joyance rest.]

Hath this been heard by thee, O Indian
    Prince!
With mind intent? hath all the ignorance—
Which bred thy trouble—vanished, My
    Arjun?

   Arjuna. Trouble and ignorance are gone!
    the Light
Hath come unto me, by Thy favor, Lord!

Now am I fixed! my doubt is fled away!
According to Thy word, so will I do!

Sanjaya. Thus gathered I the gracious
speech of Krishna, O my King!
Thus have I told, with heart a-thrill, this
wise and wondrous thing

By great Vyasa's learning writ, how Krishna's
self made known
The Yoga, being Yoga's Lord. So is the high
truth shown!

And aye, when I remember, O Lord my King,
again
Arjuna and the God in talk, and all this holy
strain,

Great is my gladness: when I muse that
splendor, passing speech,
Of Hari, visible and plain, there is no tongue
to reach

My marvel and my love and bliss. O Archer-
Prince! all hail!
O Krishna, Lord of Yoga! surely there shall
not fail

Blessing, and victory, and power, for Thy
most mighty sake,

Where this song comes of Arjun, and how
  with God he spake.

HERE ENDS, WITH CHAPTER XVIII,

Entitled "Mokshasanyasayog,"
Or "The Book of Religion by Deliverance
and Renunciation,"

THE BHAGAVAD-GITA.